i

A CHRONICLE

OF THE

FIRST THIRTEEN YEARS OF THE REIGN OF

KING EDWARD THE FOURTH,

ii

A CHRONICLE

OF THE

FIRST THIRTEEN YEARS OF THE REIGN OF

KING EDWARD THE FOURTH,

BY JOHN WARKWORTH, D.D.

MASTER OF ST. PETER'S COLLEGE, CAMBRIDGE.

EDITED, FROM THE MS. NOW IN THE LIBRARY OF ST. PETER'S COLLEGE,

BY JAMES ORCHARD HALLIWELL, ESQ. F.R.S., F.S.A.

OF JESUS COLLEGE, CAMBRIDGE; CORRESPONDING MEMBER OF THE ROYAL SOCIETY
OF ANTIQUARIES OF FRANCE, &c. &c. &c.

" Offt sithes it is seene that dyvers ther arne, the which forseene not the causis
precedent and subsequent, for the which they fall many tymes into such erroure, that
they abuse theymeself, and also othir theire sequacis, gheving credence to such as
wrigten of affeccion, leving the trouth that was in deede."—*Hearne's Fragment, p.* 293.

Facsimile reprint, 1990,
by Llanerch Enterprises.

LONDON:

PRINTED FOR THE CAMDEN SOCIETY,

BY JOHN BOWYER NICHOLS AND SON, PARLIAMENT STREET.

M.DCCC.XXXIX.

INTRODUCTION.

MR. HUNTER, in the Appendix to the last Report of the Record Commissioners,* was the first who noticed the existence of a singularly valuable and curious historical document preserved in the library of St. Peter's College, Cambridge, which had been extensively quoted by Leland in his Collectanea at the commencement of the sixteenth century. Leland extracts from a MS. volume of Chronicles given to the College by John Warkworth, who was then Master, the greater portion of which is a mere copy of Caxton's edition of the Brute Chronicle; and although, without the slightest notion of a judicious selection, that industrious transcriber has extracted as largely from the Brute as from the other part of the manuscript, yet his Collectanea has for three centuries been the only known receptacle † of a portion of the exceed-

* Fol. Lond. 1837, p. 336, col. 2.

† Previously, however, to Mr. Hunter's notice, the manuscript itself had been mentioned, but not for an historical purpose, in Mr. Hartshorne's Book Rarities of the University of Cambridge, p. 390.

ingly curious facts recorded in Warkworth's own Chronicle, and would, perhaps, have been for three centuries
longer, had not the antiquarian diligence of Mr. Hunter
discovered its latent resting-place, and added one more
to the many instances of valuable documents rescued
from oblivion by that zealous and able historian.

The following Chronicle comprises a history of the first
thirteen years of the reign of Edward the Fourth. "This
eventful period," well observes Sir Henry Ellis, "though
removed from us scarcely more than three centuries, is still
among the darkest on our annals. Its records are con-
fused, mutilated, and disjointed. They who wrote history in it, had no talents for the task ; and there was a
ferocity abroad among the partizans of both the rival
houses, which prevented many from even assembling the
materials of history."* The paucity of documents illus-
trating this period has, indeed, long † been a matter of
regret. To meet with one, then, so minute in particulars, abounding in new facts, and of indisputable au-
thenticity, cannot but be a matter of congratulation to
the historian.

It is quite unnecessary here to enlarge on the history
of the period to which the following narrative relates.
There is, however, one part of this diary, for in many

* Original Letters. Second Series, vol. i. p. 94.
† Gentleman's Magazine, 1791, vol. 61, Pt. i. p. 222.

instances it is sufficiently minute to be called an occa-
sional one, which must necessarily arrest the attention of
every reader,—the account of the mysterious death of King
Henry, expressed in such decided terms, and with such
apparently perfect knowledge of every part of the transaction, as cannot fail to raise strong doubts of its authen-
ticity. On a question of so dark a nature, no excuse will
be needed for another writer entering into the contro-
versy, with the aid of an additional auxiliary of powerful
evidence.

Before I proceed further, I will place before the reader
a few of the unpublished evidences I have collected relative to this transaction :—

1. "Obitus Regis Henrici Sexti, qui obiit *inter* vicesi-
mum primum diem Maii et xxij^m. diem Maii." MS. Bib.
Reg. 2 B. xv. fol. 1, r^o.

2. "Rex Henricus Sextus in arce Londoñ ferro trans-
figitur et occiditur." MS. Cotton. Otho, B. xiv. fol.
221, v^o.

3. "Et Henricus, nuper Rex, reponitur in Turrim
Londoñ, et, in vigilia Ascenscionis dormiente, ibidem
feliciter moriens, per Tamisiam navicula usque ad Ab-
bathiam de Cheltosye deductus, ibi sepultus est." MS.
Arundel, (College of Arms) No. 5, fol. 171, v^o.

4. "Et in vigilia ascensionis moriebatur Rex Henricus
Sextus in turri Londoniarum, qui quidem sepultus erat

apud Chersey, et postea translatus per Regem Ricardum usque Wynsowerem." MS. Laud, 674. (B. 23) fol. 11, r°.

5. There is a Latin prophecy (written perhaps after the fulfilment of the predicted event) in MS. Digb. 196, that King Henry the Sixth shall die a violent death.

6. "Also upon ascencion evyn, Kyng Henry was brought from the tower thrugh Chepe unto Powlys upon a bere, and abowte the beere more glevys and stavys than torches ; who was slayne, as it was said, by the Duke of Glowcetir ; but howe he was deed [nobody knewe, but] thedir he was brought deed ; and in the chirch the corps stode all nyght, and on the morue he was conveyed to Chertsey, where he was buryed.." MS. London Chronicle. Bibl. Cotton. Vitell. A. xvi. fol. 133, r°.

7. The following is taken from a metrical history of the reign of Edward the Fourth, by John Herd, M.D., a copy of which is in MS. Cotton. Jul. C. ii.

> " Interea Henricus Sextus, spoliatus avito
> Qui fuit imperio, vita spoliatur, in arce
> In Thamesis ripa vitreas que prospicit undas.
> Illum fama refert rigidum jugulasse Richardum,
> Gloucestrensis erat qui dux, vir sevus et audax,
> Post cujus cœdem sic insultasse refertur ;—
> ' Masculus, en ! hæres Edverdo a rege creatus,
> Tertius illius qui vixit nominis olim,
> Preter nos hodie respirat nemo superstes—
> Nos, Eboracensis quos gloria stirpis honorat !'
> Henrici corpus Pauli transfertur in ædem,
> Et jacet in feretro, vulgi ut videatur ocellis.

Parvulus est vicus, Chersei nomine notus,
In quo cœnobium, sacer Erchenwalde, locabas,
Londini fueras qui clarus episcopus olim;
Huc delatus erat tumuloque Henricus opertus;
Post Vindessoram translatus, conditur æde
Que sacrata tibi celebratur, dive Georgi!
Octo et ter denos Henricus præfuit annos;
Sex etiam menses post sceptra recepta regebat;
Vitæ annos binos et quinquaginta peregit:
Edverdus princeps gnatus fuit unicus illi.''

Fol. 170 vᵒ—171 rᵒ.

8. "Eodem die [mensis Maij xxjᵒ.] decessit Henricus Sextus, olim dictus Rex Anglie, apud Turrim Londoñ, et sepultus est in monasterio de Chertesey juxta Tamisiam Wintoñ dioces'. Et sic nemo relinquitur in humanis qui ex illo stirpite coronam petat." MS. Arundel, Mus. Brit. 28, fol. 25, vᵒ.

John Blakman*, after relating an anecdote of the patience of Henry, adds—"Consimilem etiam misericordiam cum pluribus aliis ostendit, specialiter autem duobus, mortem ei intendentibus, quorum unus collo suo grave vulnus inflixit, volens excerebrasse vel decolasse eum, quod tamen Rex patientissime tulit, dicens, *forsothe and forsothe, ye do fouly to smyte a kynge enoynted so;*" and he afterwards proceeds to state—"Et tandem mortis ibi corporis violentiam sustinuit propter regnum, et tunc spe-

---

* De virtutibus et miraculis Regis Henrici, pp. 301 et 303.

rabatur, ab aliis pacifice possidendum." Little did the author of the following curious song imagine that his reigning sovereign would arrive at so tragical an end—

> " Now grawnt him hit so be may—
> Pray we that Lord is Lord of alle,
> To save our Kyng, his reme ryalle,
> And let never myschip uppon him falle,
> Ne false traytoure him to betray.
> I praye ȝoue, seris, of ȝour gentre,
> Syng this carol reverently;
> Fore hit is mad of Kyng Herre,
> Gret ned fore him we han to pray!
> ȝif he fare wele, wele schul we be,
> Or ellis we may be ful sore;
> Fore him schul wepe mone an e,
> Thus prophecis the Blynd Awdlay."*

And " mone an e " doubtless did weep for the sainted Prince. The Croyland Continuator forcibly concludes his account with the following prayer: " may God grant time for repentance to the person, whoever he was, who laid his sacrilegious hands on the Lord's anointed."

* MS. Douce, Bib. Bodl. Oxon. No. 302, fol. 29, vᵒ, a. A folio volume on vellum containing poems by John Awdlay, the blind poet, and (fol. 22, vᵒ, b.) written in the Monastery of Haghmond in the year 1426. Mr. Hartshorne will use this MS. in his forthcoming Shropshire Glossary. I may refer here to four Latin verses on Henry the Sixth in MS. Bodl. 926. Laud, 670. E. 3. (Bern. 61.)

But to return from this digression. Mr. Bayley says "we have satisfactory testimony that Henry lived at least up to the twenty-fifth of May," and he quotes the *Fœdera* for his authority, thereby falling into an error which Sharon Turner made, in mistaking the day of the payment of certain monies for that on which they were incurred,—an error which Dr. Lingard was the first to point out, and which takes away entirely the only seeming substantial evidence that has been brought forward to show that Henry did not die between the 21st and the 22nd of May, as stated in the following Chronicle. Fleetwood's narrative affirms that Henry expired on the 23rd " of pure displeasure and melancholy," and this very palpable attempt at deception proves at any rate that the popular feeling and opinion was strong enough to induce the Yorkists to attempt to throw a veil over the important circumstantial fact that would render a murder probable, viz. that Henry died the very night Edward made his triumphal entry into the metropolis.* Indeed, the whole

---

* The catalogue of authorities for the murder of Henry VI. might be extended *ad libitum,* and do not show more than the popular opinion after all ; it may be as well, however, to give a few references. L'Art de verifier les Dates, i. 816, col. i. ; Harl. Miscell. i. 313 ; Life of Henry the Sixth (8vo. Lond. 1712), p. 58 ; Grafton's continuation of Harding's Chronicle, Sir Henry Ellis's edition, p. 460 ; " Rex Henricus occiditur clam in Turri," MS. Tanner, Bodl. II.

of the circumstantial evidence is in favour of the murder ;
Edward made his triumphal entry into London on the
21st, and went into Kent with the Duke of Gloucester on
the following day ; on the afternoon of the 22nd, Henry's
body was brought to St. Paul's, and there, as we are informed by four good authorities, *bled afresh*—

> " O, gentlemen, see, see ! dead Henry's wounds
> Open their congealed mouths, and bleed afresh !—
> Blush, blush, thou lump of foul deformity ;
> For 'tis thy presence that exhales this blood
> From cold and empty veins, where no blood dwells ;
> Thy deed, inhuman and unnatural,
> Provokes this deluge most unnatural."

William Habington* remarks that " the death of King
Henry was acted in the darke, so that it cannot be
affirmed who was the executioner, only it is probable it
was a resolution, of the state. The care of the king's
safety and the publicke quiet, in some sort making it,

fol. 104, vº. and fol. 56, rº ; Hist. Anglic. a M. H. 1640, p. 180 ;
Cooper's Chronicle, p. 267 ; MS. Harl. 2408 ; Palmesii Continuatio
Chron. Eusebiani, edit. 1483, fol. 160, rº ; Mémoires Olivier de la
Marche, sub anno 1469 ; Lilii Chronicon Angliæ, edit. 1565, fol.
63, rº ; the Breviat Chronicle of the Kings of England, edit. Cant.
1553, aº. 1470 ; MS. Viñc. in Coll. Arm. 418.

* The Historie of Edward the Fourth. Lond. 1640, p. 104.

however cruell, yet necessary ;" and he adds, " at what
time his body lay in Saint Paul's, and after in Blacke-
fryers, a large quantity of blood issued from his nose—
a most miraculous way of speaking the barbarisme of
his murther, and giving tyrants to understand that the
dead dare in their language tell the truth, and call even
their actions to account." I make this extract for the
purpose of remarking on Habington's political reason for
the murder of Henry—an argument which Hume and all
subsequent historians, with the exception of Dr. Lingard,
have strangely underrated. If the life of Henry was of
no importance, how was it that at Ludford the leader of
the Yorkists considered it expedient to report his death,
and actually cause mass to be celebrated for the repose
of his soul, although he knew that the King was then alive
and well*. Neither do I consider the argument alleged
by Sir James Mackintosh † of much weight—*it is impro-
bable that those who through so many scenes of blood
had spared the Prince should at last incur the odium of
destroying him.* Had not the most recent of Edward's
misfortunes been owing to him ? and, moreover, while
the child was living,‡ so long as the heir apparent of the

* Rot. Parl. V. 348; Owen and Blakeway's History of Shrewsbury, vol. i. p. 229.

† History of England, vol. ii. p. 44.

‡ " And shortly after [his final defeat], to make that parte sure,

throne was in existence—if so, indeed, he could be called after the treaty made by his father—the life of Henry was not worth caring for in comparison with the danger of destroying him. But now the love of the people, stronger and more enthusiastic as the unfortunate Henry was overwhelmed with greater and increasing difficulties, tended towards, and, perhaps, would ultimately have accomplished, the ejection of his rival, a sovereign who was inclined to deal heavily with them, and who never could have been a general favourite.

Warkworth informs us that the Duke of Gloucester was at the Tower of London on the night of the murder of Henry. No certain evidence has transpired relative to the share that this prince had in the deed, nor is it to be expected that we could obtain any; the voice of the people attributed the direct performance of the murder to him; and his insatiable ambition, for his road was doubtless more open after Henry's decease, afforded a fair ground for the presumption. Philip de Comines says, " if what was told me be true, after the battle was over, the Duke of Gloucester slew this poor King Herry with

was deprived of his lief, havinge loste also Edward his sonne the Prynce before spoken of, the hope of all his posteritie, in the Battayle of Tewksbury." MS. Sloan. 3479. fol. 6, v⁰. See also MS. Arundel, Mus. Brit. 28. fol. 25, v⁰. which contains the only early authority for this view of the transaction.

his own hand, or caused him to be carried to some private place, and stood by himself, while he was killed." There must have been some reason for these rumours, and De Comines was contemporary; perhaps Gloucester might have had a double purpose in the death of the king—the accomplishment of his grand aim of ambition and the service of his brother. He appears to have been detected in his aim at sovereignty, for Lewis Glyn Cothi (Works, p. 47, l. 13.) in a poem written immediately after the death of Edward, seems to have had some presentiment that Richard would succeed to the throne, for he emphatically styles him *y brenin Risiart.*

In the perusal of the following narrative every one must be struck with the difference between the characters of the two rival princes; and although, perhaps, with the enthusiasm of a staunch Lancastrian, its author has coloured the vices of the one, yet in no place has he magnified the virtues of the other. Nothing can be fairer or more sensible than the view he gives of the state of popular feeling, after the resumption of the throne by Henry.—" These were the causes, among others, which caused the people to grumble against him; and the common people said if they could have another king, he would regain all his lost possessions, and amend every corruption in the state, and bring the realm of England into prosperity and peace; nevertheless, when King Edward reigned, the people expected all the aforesaid pros-

perity and peace, but it came not; but one battle after
another, and much trouble and loss among the common
people." Almost every change, expected by the people
to produce great and immediate advantage to them, has
failed at least in its incipient operation, and the above
clearly accounts for the strong reaction in favour of
Henry. Afterwards it acted as a much more powerful
motive, and so deeply did the fortunes of the royal
prisoner excite the general compassion of his subjects,
that, after he was really deceased, no adulation was considered sufficient to sustain the well-merited reputation
of his moral virtues. Of this we have a remarkable instance in the legendary life of him, written by a monk of
Windsor about the year 1500, which opens with the
following hymn,*—

> " Salve! miles preciose,
>   Rex Henrice generose,
>   Palmes vitis celice;
>   In radice caritatis
>   Vernans flore sanctitatis,
>   Viteque angelice.
>
> " Salve! flos nobilitatis,
>   Laus et honor dignitatis,
>   Seu corone regie;

* De miraculis Henrici Sexti, libri duo. MS. Harl. 423, fol.72, rº.

Pie pater orphanorum,
Vera salus populorum,
　　Robur et ecclesie.

" Salve ! forma pietatis,
Exemplar humilitatis,
　　Decus innocencie !
Vi oppressis vel turbatis,
Mestis atque desolatis,
　　Scola paciencie.

" Salve ! fax superne lucis,
Per quam servi summi ducis
　　Illustrantur undique :
Dum virtute lucis vere,
Meruisti prefulgere
　　Tantis signis gratie.

" Salve ! quem Rex seculorum
Choris jungens angelorum
　　Civem fecit patrie ;
Te laudare cupientes
Fac ut semper sint fruentes
　　Tecum vita glorie !   Amen."

Henry the Seventh made an application to Pope Alexander the Sixth for the canonization of Henry, but his extreme penuriousness was the reason of its not being carried into effect, as he was unwilling to incur the necessary expenses.

John Lidgate's well-known poem on the Kings of England concludes with the reign of Henry VI.; but one manuscript * contains an addition relating to Edward IV. which renders the entire stanzas on those two reigns worthy of insertion, because the contrast is most singular;—

> " Sixt Henry brought forthe in al vertu,
> By just title borne by enheritaunce,
> Aforne providede by grace of Criste Jhesu,
> To were ij. crownys in Ynglonde and in Fraunce ;
> To whom Gode hathe yove soverayne suffisaunce
> Of vertuous lyfe, and chose hym for his knyghte,
> Longe to rejoyse and reigne in his righte.

> " Comforthe al thristy and drynke with gladnes !
> Rejoyse withe myrthe thoughe ye have nate to spende !
> The tyme is come to avoyden yowre distres—
> Edwarde the fourthe the olde wronges to amende
> Is wele disposede in wille, and to defende
> His londe and peple in dede, withe kynne and myghte ;
> Goode lyf and longe I pray to God hym sende,
> And that seynte George be withe hym in his righte."

It is evident that this latter part was written at the commencement of the reign of Edward IV.

The MS. which contains the Chronicle now printed

---

* MS. Harl. 2251, fol. 4, rᵒ.

consists of a folio volume of 225 leaves of vellum, the last
being pasted to the cover, and written not long after the
last mentioned event, A.D. 1473.   Leland errs in saying
that the MS. is in Warkworth's handwriting, for it is
evidently the work of a common scribe ; we fortunately
possess a note of presentation in Warkworth's autography,
and the fac-simile of this, with a specimen of the scribe's
calligraphy, will be found at the commencement of the
volume.   The sentence with which Warkworth opens his
memoranda is curious ; it is. probable that he had two
copies of Caxton's Chronicle, in one of which he had
written his own continuation, beginning with the words
" at the coronacyone of the forseyde Edward," and in the
other, instead of making a second copy of the continuation, he simply made the reference " as for alle thynges
that folowe, referre them to my copey, in whyche is
wretyn a remanente [or continuation] lyke to this forseyd
werke" [i. e. written in the same manner as Caxton's
Chronicle.]   The scribe, who made the transcript of
Caxton now preserved at Peterhouse, had been directed
to refer from one manuscript to the other for the continuation, and in so doing he added Warkworth's note of
reference by way of introduction to the new part, joining
them together by means of the words " that is to wytt,
that."
The scribe of the Brute Chronicle has exchanged Cax-

ton's orthography for his own, as the reader may readily see by comparing the printed edition with the following conclusion :—

"And here I make ane ende of this lytelle werke as myche as I can fynde aftere the forme of the werke byfore made by Ranulpd Monke of Chestere. And where ther is ony faughte I beseche them that schal rede it to correcte it. For yf I cowede have founde moo storyes I wolde have sett in itt moo; but the substaunce that I can fynde and knowe I have schortely seett them in this boke, to the entent that suche thynges as have be done sithe deythe or ende of the same booke of Polycronycone be hade in rememberaunce and not putt in oblyvione, ne forgetynge prayenge alle them that schalle see this simple werke to pardone my symple and rude wrytynge. Endede the secunde day of Julij the xxij. yere of the regne of Kynge Edwarde the fourt, and of the incarnacyone of oure Lorde M¹. cccc. iiij. score and tweyne.

"*Finysched and ended after the copey of Caxtone then in Westmynster.*" Fol. 214, v°.

For the sake of the general reader it may be as well to give the note of presentation, lithographed at the commencement of this volume, in full :—

"Liber Collegii Sancti Petri in Cantebrigia, ex dono Magistri Johannis Warkeworthe, Magistri dicti Collegii, sub interminacione anathematis nullatenus a libraria ibidem alienandus."

From the style in which this is written, there can be no doubt that it is in Warkworth's own handwriting; and it is also evident from a comparison with several of his autographs still preserved in the library of the College.

I have been able to collect nothing relative to the personal history of Warkworth, except that he was Master of St. Peter's College from A.D. 1473 to A.D. 1498.* He appears to have been a man of moderate learning and ability, although his story about the *Wemere* partakes strongly of superstition, and a reliance upon mere hearsay; but, in some instances, his minuteness in particulars would lead us to believe that he was intimately acquainted with the political affairs of the period.

The account which he gives of Henry's death is certainly most singular. It would seem as if he had intended for every reader a certain assurance far from being voluntarily taken—

* In St. Peter's College there is an original picture of Warkeworthe, executed in 1498, in a clerical habit, holding an open book with both his hands. This was formerly in the curious room called the Stone Parlour, but is now, I believe, transferred to the library. There is the following distich underneath—

> " Vives adoptata gaudeto prole ; probato
> Non cuicunque libet, progenuisse licet."

In the ancient register of donations to the College is a list of

" Rede this treyte it may hym move—
And may hym tecbe lightly with awe."*

Be that as it may, Warkworth's narrative is supported by
the strongest collateral proof, and is therefore deserving
of the greatest consideration.

I may observe that much new matter to illustrate this
period may be found in the contemporary poems of Lewis
Glyn Cothi, a Welsh bard, part of whose works have lately
been published by the Royal Cymmrodorion Institution,
under the able editorship of my friend the Rev. John
Jones, M.A. (Tegid), of Christ Church, Oxford, and the
Rev. W. Davies. I have made more particular reference
to these spirited poems in the notes; but I take the opportunity here of pointing out to the general reader Mr.
Jones's Introductory Essay on the Wars of the Rival
Roses, which would have done ample credit to a work
professing far higher pretensions: I speak of it not as
the result of much research, or of any difficult research
whatever, but as being an admirable view of the facts of
the case, discussed with great judgment and ability, and

books given to the library by Warkeworthe, and from this it appears
that he presented his MS. Chronicle in the year 1483.

* MS. Bodl. 3692. Hyp. Bodl. 160. (226.) Tract. sep. ult. fol.
1, rº. *A miracle play of the Burial of Christ, of the fifteenth century.*
I quote this MS. for the purpose of pointing out a curious miracle-
play which does not appear to have been hitherto known.

well adapted to fulfil the purpose for which it was intended.

———

I gladly take the opportunity of expressing my respect-
ful and grateful thanks to the Rev. William Hodgson,
D.D., Master of St. Peter's College, and Vice-Chancellor
of the University of Cambridge, for the readiness with
which I have been favoured with every possible facility
for rendering the text of the following document as correct as the MS. will allow.

I also beg leave to return my best thanks to Charles
George Young, Esq., York Herald, for the extreme kindness and liberality with which he assisted some researches
I found it expedient to make in the library of the College of Arms ; and to John Gough Nichols, Esq. for the
communication of some valuable observations, which will
be found introduced among the notes under his initials,
and for the comprehensive index to the text and notes.
The correctness of the printed text has been ensured by
a careful collation made by Mr. Black, whose experience
in these matters has rendered his assistance most valuable.

                              JAMES O. HALLIWELL.

35, Alfred Place, Sept. 18th, 1839.

Fac-Simile from the first page of Warkworth's Chronicle.

Note on the cover of the Volume.

WARKWORTH'S CHRONICLE.

As FOR alle thynges that folowe, referre them to my copey, in whyche is wretyn a remanente lyke to this forseyd werke: that is to wytt, that, at the coronacyone of the forseyde Edwarde, he create and made dukes his two brythir, the eldere George Duke of Clarence, and his yongere brothir Richard Duke of Gloucetre; and the Lord Montagu, the Erle of Warwykes brothere, the Erle of Northumberlonde; and one William Stafford squiere, Lord Stafforde of Southwyke; and Sere Herbard, Lorde Herbard, and aftere Lorde Erle of Penbroke; and so the seide Lorde Stafforde was made Erle of Devynschire; the Lorde Gray Ryffyne, Erle of Kent; the Lorde Bourchyer, Erle of Essex; the Lorde Jhon of Bokyngham, the Erle of Wyltschyre; Sere Thomas Blount, knyghte, Lord Mont[joy]; Sere Jhon Hawarde, Lorde Hawarde; William Hastynges he made Lorde Hastynges and grete Chamberlayne; and the Lorde Ryvers; Denham squyere, Lorde Dynham; and worthy as is afore schewed; and othere of gentylmen and yomenne he made knyghtes and squyres, as thei hade desserved.

And also the fyrst yere of his regne he ordeyned a parleament, at whiche were atteynted Kynge Herry and all othere that fledde with hym into Scotlonde oute of Englonde; and for so moche as he

fande in tyme of nede grete comforth in his comyners, he ratyfied
and confermyd alle the ffraunsches yeve to citeis and townes, &c.
and graunted to many cyteis and tounes new fraunschesses more
than was graunted before, ryghte largly, and made chartours therof
to the entent to have the more good wille and love in his londe.

Also Quene Margrett, Herry Duke of Excetre, the Duke of Somersett, and other lordes that fleede Englonde, hade kepte certeyne
castelles in Northumberlond, as Awnwyk, Bambrught, Dunstone-
brught, and also Werworthe, whiche they hade vytaled and stuffed
bothe with Englischemenne, Frenschemenne, and Scottesmenne; by
the whiche castelle[s] thei hade the moste party of alle Northumberlond.   Kynge Edwarde and his counselle, thynkynge and un [der]
stondynge wat hurte myghte appene thereof, made commyssiones to
the sowthe and west cowntre, and hade of them gret money, wyth the
whiche menne made redy, and beseged the same castelle[s] in the
moneth of Decembre in the yere aforseide.   And Sere Peris le Brasylle, knyght, of Fraunce, and the best warrer of alle that tyme, was
in Scotlonde to helpe Quene Margaret; when he knew that the
castelles were besegede, he hade xx m¹. of Scottesmenne, and came
toward Alnwyke and alle the other castels.   And whenne Kynge
Edwardes hooste had knowlege that Sere Perys le Brasille with the
Scottesmenne were comynge, thei remewed from the sege and were
affrayed; and the Scottesche hoost supposed it hade be doone for
some gayne, and thei were affrayed; also thei durst noȝt come
neghe the castelle; for and thei hade comyne one boldly, thei
myghte have takyne and distressit alle the lordes and comeners, for
thei hade lye ther so longe in the felde, and were greved with colde
and rayne, that thei hade no coreage to feght, &c.   Never the lattere
whenne thei that were in the castelle beseged saw that the sege was
withedraw for fere, and the Scottes host afferde, also thei came
oute of the castelle and lefte them opene, &c.; and so afterwarde
Kynge Edwardes hoost enterde into alle the hole castelle, and kept
it, &c.

And after that, the castelle of Bamburght was yoldene to the Kynge, by treyatte and apoyntment by Herry the Duke of Somersett that kept it, and came in to Kynge Edwardes grace, whiche graunted to hym a M^l. marke by yere, whereof he was not payede; the[r]for he departed oute of Englonde after halff yere into Scotlonde, &c. And so Kynge Edward was possessed of alle Englonde, excepte a castelle in Northe Wales called Harlake, whiche Sere Richard Tunstall kepte, the qwhiche was gotene afterwarde by the Lorde Harberde.

And in the thyrde yere of the reygne of Kynge Edwarde, and anno Domini M°.cccc.lxiij, ther was ane fervent froste thrugh Englonde, and snowe, that menne myght goo overe the yise, and a fervent colde. And also ther was holde a parleamente at Westmynster, in the whiche was graunted to the Kynge ane ayde, whiche was as moche money as the xv. parte of mennys goodes and ane halff so myche more, where of the peple grocchede sore.

Also the iiij^e yere of Kynge Edwarde, the Erle of Warwyke was sent into Fraunce for a maryage for the Kynge, for one fayre ladye, suster-doughtere to the Kynge of Fraunce, whiche was concludede by the Erle of Warwyke. And whiles the seyde Erle of Warwyke was in Fraunce, the Kynge was wedded to Elisabethe Gray, wedow, the qwiche Sere Jhon Gray that was hyre housbonde was slayne at Yorke felde in Kynge Herry partye; and the same Elisabeth was doughtere to the Lorde Ryvers; and the weddynge was prevely in a secrete place, the fyrst day of Maye the yere above seide. And when the Erle of Warwyke come home and herde hereof, thenne was he gretely displesyd withe the Kyng; and after that rose grete discencyone evere more and more betwene the Kyng and hym, for that and other, &c. And thenne the Kyng put oute of the Chaunceler-schepp the Bysshope of Excetre, brother to the Erle of Warwyke, and made the Bysshoppe of Bathe Chaunceler of Englonde. After that the Erle of Warwyke toke to hyme in fee as many knyghtys, squyers, and gentylmenne as he myght, to be stronge; and Kyng Edwarde dide that he myght to feble the Erles powere. And yett thei were acorded diverse tymes: but thei nevere loffyd togedere aftere.

Also in the iiij^{te} yere of the Kynge Edwarde, the monethe of Maij, the Duke of Somersett, the Lorde Roos, the Lorde Moleyns, Talboys the Erle of Kyme, Sire Phylippe Wenterworth, Sire Thomas Fynderne, gadred a grete peple of the northe contre. And Sere Jhon Nevelle, that tyme beynge Erle of Northumberlonde, with x. ml. men come uppon them, and there the comons fleede that were with them, and ther the forseide lordes were takene and afterward behedede. But thenne the Lorde Montagu, the Erle of Warwykes brothere, whiche the Kynge had made Erle of Northumberlonde, was myghty and stronge by the same, &c. And for so moche as the Kynge and his counselle thought that he wolde holde with his Erle of Warwyke, therfor the Kyng and his counselle made the countre to desire that thei myght have the ryghtfull heyre Percy, sonne to Henry Percy that was slayne at Yorke Feld, to be the Erle of Northumberlond; and so it was doone. And aftere this the Kynge made Lorde Montagu, Marquyus Montagu, and made his sonne Duke of Bedford, whiche schulde wedde the princesse, the Kynges heldest doughter, whiche, by possibylite, schuld be Kynge of Englonde; and so he hade many fayre wordys and no lordeschyppys, but alwey he promysed he wuld do, &c.

Also the same yere, and the yere of oure Lord Ml.cccc.lxiiij. Kynge Edwarde chaunged the coyne of Englonde, by whiche he hade grete getynge; for he made of ane olde noble a ryall, the whiche was commaundyde to goo for x.s.; nevere the latter the same ryolle was put viij.d. of aley, and so weyed viij.d. more by delaynge; and smote hym in to a newe prynte. Also he made of iij.d. a grote; and also he [made] angelle noblys of vj.s. viij.d., and by diverse coynes, to the grete harme of the comene peple.

Also the same yere, Kynge Herry was takene bysyde a howse of religione in Lancaschyre, by the mene of a blacke monke of Abyngtone, in a wode called Cletherwode, besyde Bungerly Hyppyngstones, by Thomas Talbott, sonne and heyre to Sere Edmunde Talbot of Basshalle, and Jhon Talbott his cosyne of Colebry, withe other moo; whiche disseyvide, beyngne at his dynere at Wadyngtone Halle, and caryed to Londone on horse bake, and his lege bownde to the styrope, and so brought thrugh Londone to the Toure, where he was kepte longe tyme by two squyres and ij. yomen of the crowne, and ther menne; and every manne was suffred to come and speke withe hym, by licence of the kepers.

And in the vth yere of Kynge Edwarde, the Erle of Oxenforde, the Lord Abrey his sonne, and Sere Thomas Todenam knyght, were taken, and brought into the Toure of Londone, and there was leyde to them hye tresone; and aftyrwarde thei were brought before the Erle of Worscetre, and juged by lawe padowe that thei schuld be hade to the Toure Hylle, where was made a scaffolde of viij. fote hy3t, and ther was there hedes smyten of, that alle menne myght see; whereof the moste peple were sory.

And in the vi. yere of Kynge Edwarde regne, the Lorde Hungerforde was takene and behedede for hye treasoune at Salisbury. And in vij. yere of Kynge Edwarde, Sere Thomas Cooke, Sere Jhon Plummere, knyght, and aldermenne of Londone, and Humfrey Haward and other aldermen were arested, and treasoune surmysed uppone them, whereof thei were acquyte, but thei lost grete goodes to the Kynge, to the valowe of xl. M^l. marke or more; and diverse tymes in dyverse places of Englonde, men were arestede for treasoune, and some were putt to dethe, and some scaped.

And the viij. yere of the regne of Kynge Edwarde, a lytelle before Michaelmasse, there apperyde a blasynge sterre in the weste, a iiij. fote hyghe by estymacyone, in evenynge, goynge fro the weste

towarde the northe, and so endurede v. or vj. wekes. And the
same yere Sere Thomas Hungerforde knyght, sonne to the Lorde
Hungerforde, and Herry Curteney, the Erle of Devynschyre of
right, were takene for treasoune and behedede at Salisbury; and
menne seyde the Lorde Stafforde of Southwyke was cause of the
seyde Herry Curtenayes dethe, for he wolde be the Erle of Devynschyre, and so the Kynge made hym afterwarde, and [he] hade it
noȝt halff a yere.

And in the ix. yere of the regne of Kynge Edwarde, at mysso-
mere, the Duke of Clarence passede the see to Caleis to the Erle
of Warwyke, and there weddede his doughter by the Archebysshoppe of Yorke the Erle of Warwyke brothere, and afterwarde
come overe ayene. And anone aftere that, by ther assig[n]ment,
there was a grete insurreccyon in Yorkeschyre, of dyvers knyghtes,
squyres, and comeners, to the nowmbere of xx^{ti} м^l.; and Sere
William Conyars knyghte was therre capteyne, whiche callede
hym self Robyne of Riddesdale; and agens them aroose, by the
Kynges commawndement, Lorde Harbarde, Erle of Penbroke,
withe xliij. м^l. of Walschemenne, the beste in Wales, and Humfray
Stafforde, with vij. м^l. of archers of the weste countre; and as
thei went togedere to mete the northemenne at a towne, there
felle in a varyaunce for ther logynge, and so the Erle of Deven-
schyre departed from the Erle of Penbroke withe alle his menne.
And Robyne of Riddesdale came uppone the Walschemenne in
a playne byyonde Banbury toune, and ther thei faughthe strongly
togedere, and ther was the Erle of Penbroke takene, and his brother
withe hym, and two м^l. Walschmenne slayne, and so the Walsch-
men loste the felde the xxvj. day of Juylle the same yere. The
names of the gentylmen that were slayne of Walsche party in the
same batelle:—Sere Rogere Vaghan, knyght; Herry Organ sonne
and heyre; Thomas Aprossehere Vaghan, squyere; William Harbarde of Breknoke, squyere; Watkyn Thomas, sonne to Rogere

Vaghan; Yvan ap Jhon of Merwyke; Davy ap Jankyn of Lym̄-
meryke; Harry Done ap Pikton; John Done of Kydwelle; Ryse
ap Morgon ap Ulston; Jankyn Perot ap Scottesburght; John
Eneand of Penbrokeschire; and Jhon Contour of Herforde. And
of the north party ther was slayne Sere Herry Latymere, sonne and
heyre to the Lorde Latymere; Sere Rogere Pygot, knyghte; James
Conya[r]s, sonne and heyre to Sere Jhon Conya[r]s, knyght;
Olivere Audley, squyere; Thomas Wakes sonne and heyre; William
Mallerye, squyere; and many othere comyners, &c. And at that
tyme was the Lorde Ryvers takene, and one of his sonnes, in the
forest of Dene, and brought to Northamtone, and the Erle of Penbroke a[nd] Sere Richard Herbarde his brother were behedede at
Northamtone, alle iiij. by the commawndement of the Duke of
Clarence and the Erle of Warwyke; and Thomas Harbarde was
slayne at Brystow, &c. And at that same tyme was Stafford, that was
Erle of Devynschyre but half a yere, take at Bryggewatere by the
comons ther in Somersettschyre, and ther ryghte behedede. And
after that the Archebysschoppe of Yorke had understondynge that
Kynge Edwarde was in a vilage bysyde Northamptone, and alle his
peple he reysyd were fledde fro hym; by the avyse of the Duke
of Clarence and the Erle of Warwyke he rode with certeyne hors-
menne harneysed withe hym, and toke Kynge Edwarde, and had
hym unto Warwyke castelle a lytelle whyle, and afterwarde to Yorke
cite; and ther, by fayre speche and promyse, the Kynge scaped
oute of the Bisshoppys handes, and came unto Londone, and dyd
what hym lykede. And the same yere, the xxix. day of Septembre,
Humfrey Nevylle, knyght, and Charles his brothere, were takene
by the Erle of Warwyke, and behedede at Yorke, the Kynge beynge
present. And in the same yere [was] made a proclamacyone at the
Kynges Benche in Westmynstere, and in the cyte of Londone, and
in alle Englond, a generalle pardone tylle alle manere of men for
alle manere insurreccyons and trespasses; and also a hole xv^{sim}.

schulde be gaderyd and payed that same yere at Martynmasse, and at oure Lady-Day in Lent after ; whiche noyed the peple, for thei had payed a lytelle before a gret taske, and the xv. parte of every mannes good, &c.

And in the x. yere of Kynge Edwardes regne, in the moneth of Marche, the Lorde Willowby, the Lorde Welles his sonne, Thomas Delalond knyght, and Sere Thomas Dymmoke knyght, the Kynges Champyon, droff oute of Lyncolneschyre Sere Thomas à Burghe, a knyght of the Kynges howse, and pullede downe his place, and toke alle his goodes and cataylle that thei myghte fynde, and thei gaderid alle the comons of the schyre to the nowmbre of xxx. M^l., and cryed " Kynge Herry," and refused Kynge Edwarde. And the Duke of Clarence and the Erle of Warwyke causede alle this, lyke as thei dyde Robyne of Riddesdale to ryse afore that at Banbury felde. And whenne Kynge Edwarde herde hereof, he made oute his commyssyons, and gaderyd a grete peple of menne, and sent his pardone to the Lorde Wyllowby, and a commaundement that thei schuld come to hym, and so he dyd. And whenne the Kynge was sure of hym, he and alle his oste went towarde Lyncolneschyre, the Lord Welles, and alle the othere peple were gaderd togedere, and commawndede Lorde Wyllowby to sende a lettere to hys sonne and to alle the peple that he gaderyde, that thei schulde yelde them to hym as to ther sovereyne Lorde, or ellys he made a woue that the Lorde Willowby schuld lese his hede ; and he wrote and sent his lettere forthe, but therfor they wulde noȝt ceysse ; wherfor the Kynge comawndyde the Lorde Wyllowhby hede for to be smytene of, notwithstondynge his pardone. And so the Kynge toke his oste and went towarde his enemyes, and losyde his gonnys of his ordynaunce uppone them, and faught with them, and anone the comons fledde away ; but ther was many manne slayne of Lyncolneschyre, and the Lorde Wellys, Sere Thomas Delalonde, and Sere Thomas Dymmoke, knyghtys, takene and beheddede.   And whenne the Duke of Clarence and the Earl of Warwike herde the felde was loste, and how there cownselle was dyscoverede, thei fledde westwarde to the see syde, and toke there here schippys, and sayled towarde Southamptone, and e[n]tendet there to have a grete schyppe of the seide Erle of Warwykes, callyde the Trinite; but the Lorde Scales, the Quenes brother, was sent thedere by the Kynges commawndement, and other withe hym, and faught with the seide Duke and Erle, and toke there dyverse schyppes of theres and many of ther men therein; so that the Duke and the Erle were fayne to flee to the Kynge of Fraunce, where thei were worschipfully receyved.   And after this the Kynge Edwarde came to Southamptone, and commawndede the Erle of Worcetere to sitt and juge suche menne as were taken in the schyppes, and so xx. persones of gentylmen and yomenne were hangede, drawne, and quartered, and hedede ; and after that thei hanged uppe by the leggys, and a stake made scharpe at bothe endes, whereof one ende was putt in att bottokys, and the other ende ther heddes were putt uppe one ; for the whiche the peple of the londe were gretely displesyd; and evere afterwarde the Erle of Worcestre was gretely behatede emonge the peple, for ther dysordinate dethe that he used, contrarye to the lawe of the londe.

And whenne the seide Duke of Clarence and the Erle of Warwyke were in Fraunce, there apperede a blasynge sterre in the weste, and the flame therof lyke a spere hede, the whiche dyverse of the Kynges house sawe it, whereof thei were fulle sore adrede.   And thanne in Fraunce whenne the seide lordes where, thei toke there counselle qwhat was beste for to do; and thei coude fynde no remedy but to sende to Quene Margaret, and to make a maryage betwex Prynce Edwarde, Kynge Herry sonne, and an other of the seid Erle of Warwikys doughters, whiche was concluded, and in Fraunce worschippfully wedded.   And there it was apoyntede and acordede that Kynge Herry schuld rejoyse the kyngdome of

Englonde ageyne, and regne as welle as he dyd before, and after hym hys Prynce Edward and his heyres of his body lawfully begotyne; and if it appenede that he disceysed witheoute heyres of his body lawfully gotene, thenne schulde the kyngdome of Englonde, with the lordschyppes of Irlonde, remane unto George, the Duke of Clarence, and his heyre[s] for evere more. Also it was apoyncted and agreede that Herry Duke of Excetre, Edmunde Duke of Somersett, brother to Herry that was slayne at Hexham felde, the Erle of Devynschire called Courtnay, and alle othere knyghtes, squyers, and alle other that were putt oute and atayntede for Kynges Herry quarrelle, schulde come into Englonde ageyne, and every man to rejoyse his owne lyflode and inhabytauntes; whiche alle this poyntment aforeseide were wrytene, indentyde, and sealede, bytwixe the seide Quene Margaret, the Prynce hire sonne, in that one party, and the Duke of Clarence, and the Erle of Warwik, one that othere party. And moreovere, to make it sure, thei were sworne, and made grete othys eche to othere, wiche was done be alle Kynge of Fraunce counselle.

And in the same x. yere aforeseide, a lytelle before Michaelmesse, the Duke of Clarence and the Erle of Warwyke londede in the west countre, and gadered there a grete peple. The Lorde Markes Montagu hade gaderyd vi. м¹. men, by Kynge Edwardes commysyone and commaundement, to the entente to have recistede the seide Duke of Clarence, and the Erle of Warwyke. Nevere the lattere, the seide Markes Montagu hatyde the Kynge, and purposede to have taken hym; and whenne he was withein a myle of Kynge Edwarde, he declarede to the peple that was there gaderede with hym, how Kynge Edwarde hade fyrst yevyne to hym the erledome of Northumberlonde, and how he toke it from hym and gaff it Herry Percy, whos fadere was slayne at Yorke felde; and how of late tyme hade he made hym Markes of Montagu, and yaff a pyes neste to mayntene his astate withe: wherefor he yaff

knoleage to his peple that he wulde holde withe the Erle of Warwyke, his brothere, and take Kynge Edwarde if he myght, and alle
tho that wolde holde with hym.   But anone one of the oste went
oute frome the fellawschippe, and tolde Kynge Edwarde alle manere
of thynge, and bade hym avoyde, for he was no3t stronge enoghe
to gyff batayle to Markes Montagu; and then anone Kynge Edwarde
haysted hym in alle that he myght to the towne of Lynne, and ther
he toke schyppynge one Michaelmesse day, in the x. yere of his
regne, with Lorde Hastynges, that was the Kynges Chamberleyne,
Lorde Say, withe dyverse other knyghtes and squyers, passed and
saylede overe the see into Flaunders, to his brother-in-lawe the
Duke of Burgeyne, for socoure and helpe, &c.

Here is to knowe, that in the begynnynge of the moneth of Oc-
tobre, the yere of oure Lorde a M.cccc.lxx, the Bisshoppe of Wyn-
chestere, be the assent of the Duke of Clarence and the Erle of
Warwyke, went to the toure of Londone, where Kynge Herry was
in presone by Kynge Edwardes commawndement, and there toke
hyme from his kepers, whiche was no3t worschipfully arayed as a
prince, and no3t so clenly kepte as schuld seme suche a Prynce;
thei hade hym oute, and newe arayed hym, and dyde to hyme grete
reverens, and brought hyme to the palys of Westmynster, and so
he was restorede to the crowne ageyne, and wrott in alle his lettres,
wryttes, and other recordes, the yere of his regne, *Anno regni Regis
Henrici Sexti quadragesimo nono, et readempcionis sue regie potes-
tatis primo.* Whereof alle his goode lovers were fulle gladde, and the
more parte of peple.   Nevere the lattere, before that, at he was putt
oute of his reame by Kynge Edwarde, alle Englonde for the more
partye hatyd hym, and were fulle gladde to have a chounge; and the
cause was, the good Duke of Glouceter was put to dethe, and Jhon
Holonde, Duke of Excetre, poysond, and that the Duke of Suffolke,
the Lorde Say, Danyelle Trevyliane, and other myscheves pepie
that were aboute the Kynge, were so covetouse towarde them selff,

and dyde no force of the Kynges honour, ne of his wele, ne of the comone wele of the londe, where Kynge Herry trusted to them that thei schuld do, and labour in tyme of innocence evere for the comone wele, whiche thei dyde contrary to his wille; and also Fraunce, Normandy, Gasgoyne, and Guyane was lost in his tyme. And these were the causes, withe other, that made the peple to gruge ageyns hym, and alle bycause of his fals lordes, and nevere of hym; and the comon peple seyde, yf thei myghte have another Kynge, he schulde gett alle ageyne and amende alle manere of thynges that was amysse, and brynge the reame of Englond in grete prosperite and reste. Nevere the lattere, whenne Kynge Edwarde iiijth regnede, the peple looked after alle the forseide prosperytes and pecce, but it came not; but one batayle aftere another, and moche troble and grett losse of goodes amonge the comone peple; as fyrste, the xv. of alle there goodes, and thanne ane hole xv., at yett at every batell to come ferre oute there countreis at ther awne coste; and these and suche othere brought Englonde ryght lowe, and many menne seyd that Kynge Edwarde hade myche blame for hurtynge marchandyse, for in his dayes thei were not in other londes, nore wit hein Englonde, take in suche reputacyone and credence as thei were afore, &c.

And xxvj. day of Novembre, Kynge Herry callede a parleament at Westmynster, beynge there George the Archebysshoppe of Yorke, Chaunceler of Englonde, whiche [discussed] this proposicion before the Kynge and his Lordes and the comons of that same parleament assemblede, *Revertimini ad me filii revertentes, ego enim vir vester. Jeremie tercio, etc.* And in the moneth of Februarij after, Herry Duke of Excetre, Eadmunde Duke of Somersett, Lorde Jhon of Somersett his brothir, Erle of Ormond, Jasper Erle of Penbroke, brother to the Kynge Herry, and the Erle of Richmonde, with many other knyghtys, and squyres, gentilmen, and yomen, came into Englonde, and entered into ther lordschippys and londe, whiche at the parleament above seide and alle other attaynderes that were made in

Kynge Edwardys tyme were anullede, and Kynge Herry was amittèd to his crowne and dignite ageyne, and alle his men to there enherytaunce. And thenne was takene the Erle of Worcetre, whiche was arested and areynede befor Sere Jhon Veere, the Erle of Oxenforde, sonne and heyre to the forseide Erle of Oxenforde whiche was behedede at the Toure Hille, as before wrytene; and so the Erle of Worcetre was juged be suche lawe as he dyde to other menne; and, whenne he was dede, his body and his hede was buryede togedyr at the Blacke Frerys in Londone, with alle the honoure and worschyppe that his frendes coude do. Also Quene Elisabeth, Kynge Edwardes wyf, wiche hade welle vetelede and fortifyed the Toure of Londone, when sche herde that here soevereyne and husbonde was fledde, sche went secretly oute of the toure in to sanctuary at Westmynster, with alle here childrene, and sche hir selff was grete withe childe, and was delyverede ther ryght of a sonne that was callede Prynce Edwarde of Englonde; and ther sche abode stylle in grete troble, tylle Kynge Edwarde came in ageyne tylle hire.

And in the secunde weke of Marche, the xlix. yere of the regne of Kynge Herry the vj^{te}, and in the x. yere of the regne of Kynge Edwarde the iiij^{te}, the same Kynge Edwarde toke his schippynge in Flaunders, and hade withe hym the Lorde Hastynges and the Lorde Say, and ix. c. of Englismenne and three hundred of Flemmynges with hande-gonnes, and sailed toward Englonde, and hade grete troble uppon the see with stormys, and lost a schyppe withe horse; and purpost to have londede in Northfolke, and one of the Erle [of] Oxenfordes brother withe the comons of the cuntre arose up togedere, and put hym abake to the see ageyne. And after that, at he was so trobled in the see, that he was fayne to londe in Yorkeschyre at Ravenys-spore; and there rose ageyns hym alle the cuntre of Holdernes, whose capteyne was a preste, and a persone in the same cuntre called Sere Jhon Westerdale, whiche aftyrwarde for his abused disposycion was casten in presone in the

Marchalse at Londone by the same Kynge Edwarde : for the same preste mett Kynge Edwarde and askede the cause of his landynge ; and he answeryde that he came thedere by the Erle of Northumberlondes avyse, and schewede the Erles lettere y-send to hym, &c. undere his seale; and also he came for to clayme the Duchery of Yorke, the whiche was his inherytaunce of ryght, and so passed forthe to the cite of Yorke, where Thomas Clyfford lete hym inne, and ther he was examynede ayenne; and he seyde to the mayre and aldermenne and to alle the comons of the cite, in likewyse as he was afore in Holdernes at his landyng : that was to sey, that [he] nevere wulde clayme no title, ne take uppone honde to be Kynge of Englonde, nor wulde have do afore that tyme, but be excitynge and sturing of the Erle of Warwyke; and therto afore alle peple, he cryed " A ! Kynge Herry ! A ! Kynge and Prynce Edwarde ! " and wered ane estryche feder, Prynce Edwardes lyvery. And after this he was sufferd to passe the cite, and so helde his wey southwarde, and no man lettyd hym ne hurtyde hym.

Afterwarde that, he came towarde Notyngham, and ther came to hym Sere William a Stanley with ccc. men, and Sere William Norys, and dyverse other menne and tenauntes of Lorde Hastynges, so that he hade M^l. M^l. menne and moo ; and anone aftere he made his proclamacyone, and called hym self Kynge of Englonde and of Fraunce. Thenne toke he his wey to Leycetre, where were the Erle of Warwyke and the Lord Markes his brother with iiij. M^l. menne or moo. And Kynge Edwarde sent a messyngere to them, that yf thai wulde come oute, that he wulde feght withe them. But the Erle of Warwyke hade a letter from the Duke of Clarence, that he schulde not feght withe hym tylle he came hym self; and alle was to the distruccion of the Erle of Warwyke, as it happenede aftyrwarde. Yet so the Erle of Warwyke kept stille the gates of the toune schet, and suffrede Kynge Edwarde passe towarde Londone ; and a litelle oute of Warwyke mett the Duke of Clarence with Kynge Edwarde, with vij. M^l. men, and ther thei were made acorde, and made a proclamacion forthe-withe in Kynge Edwardes name; and so alle covandes of fydelite, made betwyx the Duke of Clarence, and the Erle of Warwyke, Quene Margarete, Prince Edwarde hir sonne, bothe in Englonde and in Fraunce, were clerly brokene and forsakene of the seide Duke of Clarence; whiche, in conclusione, was distruccion bothe to hym and them: for perjury schall nevere have better ende, witheoute grete grace of God. *Vide finem, &c.*

Kyng Herry thenne was in Londone, and the Archebysshoppe of Yorke, withein the Bysschoppys of Londone palece. And on the wennysday next before Ester-day, Kynge Herry and the Arche-bysschoppe of Yorke with hym roode aboute Londone, and desirede the peple to be trew unto hym; and every manne seide thei wulde. Nevere the latter, Urswyke, recordere of Londone, and diverse alder-men, suche that hade reule of the cyte, commaundede alle the peple that were in harnes, kepynge the cite and Kynge Herry, every manne to goo home to dynere; and in dyner tyme Kynge Edwarde was late in, and so went forthe to the Bisshoppes of Londone palece, and ther toke Kynge Herry and the Archebisschoppe of Yorke, and put theme in warde, the thursday next before Ester-day. And the Archebysschoppe of Cawnterbury, the Erle of Essex, the Lorde Barnesse, and suche other as awyde Kynge Edwarde good wylle, as welle in Londone as in othere places, made as many menne as thei myghte in strengthynge the seide Kynge Edwarde; so then he was a vij. M^l. menne, and ther thei refresched welle them self alle that day, and good frydai. And upone Ester evyne, he and alle his oste went toward Barnett, and caryede Kynge Herry withe hym: for he hade understondyng that the Erle of Warwycke and the Duke of Excetre, the Lorde Markes Montagu, the Erle of Oxenforde, and many other knyghtes, squyers, and comons, to the nombre of xx. M^l., were gaderide togedere to feghte ageyne Kynge

Edwarde. But it happenede that he withe his oste were en-
terede into the tounc of Barnet, before the Erle of Warwyke and
his host. And so the Erle of Warwyke and his host lay witheoute
the towne alle nyght, and eche of them loosede gonnes at othere,
alle the nyght. And on Ester day in the mornynge, the xiiij. day
of Apryl, ryght erly, eche of them came uppone othere ; and ther
was suche a grete myste, that nether of them myght see othere
perfitely ; ther thei faughte, from iiij. of clokke in the mornynge
unto x. of clokke the fore-none. And dyverse tymes the Erle of
Warwyke party hade the victory, and supposede that thei hade
wonne the felde. But it hapenede so, that the Erle of Oxenfordes
men hade uppon them ther lordes lyvery, bothe before and behynde,
which was a sterre withe stremys, wiche [was] myche lyke Kynge
Edwardes lyvery, the sunne with stremys ; and the myste was so
thycke, that a manne myghte not profytely juge one thynge from
anothere ; so the Erle of Warwikes menne schott and faughte ayens
the Erle of Oxenfordes menne, wetynge and supposynge that thei
hade bene Kynge Edwardes menne ; and anone the Erle of Oxenforde and his menne cryed "treasoune ! treasoune !" and fledde
awaye from the felde withe viij. c. menne. The Lorde Markes
Montagu was agreyde and apoyntede with Kynge Edwarde, and put
uppone hym Kynge Edwardes lyvery ; and a manne of the Erles of
Warwyke sawe that, and felle uppone hyme, and kyllede hym.
And whenne the Erle of Warwyke sawe his brothere dede, and
the Erle of Oxenforde fledde, he lepte one horse-backe, and
flede to a wode by the felde of Barnett, where was no waye
forthe ; and one of Kynge Edwardes menne hade espyede hyme,
and one came uppone hym and kylled hym, and dispolede hyme
nakede. And so Kynge Edwarde gate that felde. And ther was
slayne of the Erle of Warwykes party, the Erle hym self, Markes
Montagu, Sere William Tyrelle, knyghte, and many other. The
Duke of Excetre faugth manly ther that day, and was gretely

despolede and woundede, and lefte nakede for dede in the felde, and so lay ther from vij. of clokke tille iiij. after none ; whiche was take up and brought to a house by a manne of his owne; and a leche brought to hym, and so afterwarde brought in to sancuarij at Westmynster. And one Kynge Edwardes party was slayne the Lorde Crowmwelle, sonne and heyre to the Erle of Essex, Lord Barnes sonne and heyre, Lorde Say, and dyverse other, to the nombre (of bothe partys) iiij. M¹. menne. And after that the felde was don, Kynge Edwarde commaundyd bothe the Erle of Warwikes body and the Lord Markes body to be putt in a carte, and returned hym with alle his oste ageyne to Londone; and there commaundede the seide ij. bodyes to be layede in the chyrche of Paulis, one the pavement, that every manne myghte see them; and so they lay iij. or iiij. days, and afterwarde where buryede. And Kynge Herry, beynge in the forwarde durynge the batbaylle, was not hurt; but he was broughte ageyne to the Toure of Londone, ther to be kept.

And Quene Marget, and Prince Edwarde hire sonne, with other knygtes, squyres, and other menne of the Kyng of Fraunce, hade navy to brynge them to Englond: whiche, whenne thei were schipped in Fraunce, the wynde was so contrary unto them xvij. dayes and nyghtes, that [thei] myght not come from Normandy with unto Englonde, whiche withe a wynd myght have seylede it in xij. oures ; whiche at the xvij. dayes ende one Ester day at the evyne the[i] landed at Weymouthe, and so by lande from Weymouthe the[i] roode to Excetre; and mette withe hire, at Weymouth, Edmunde Duke of Somersett, the Lorde Jhon his brother, brother to Herry Duke of Somerset slayne at Exham, and Curteney the Erle of Devynschyre, and many othere. And on Ester mounday was brought tithingys to them, that Kynge Edwarde hade wonne the felde at Barnett, and that Kynge Herry was put into the Toure ayene. And anone ryghte thei made oute commaundementes, in the Quenes name and the Prynce, to alle the weste

countre, and gaderet grete peple, and kepte hire wey towarde the
toune of Brystow. And when the Kynge herd that thei were
landede, and hade gaderede so myche peple, he toke alle his hoste,
and went oute of Londone the wennysday in Ester weke, and
manly toke his waye towarde them; and Prynce Edwarde herd
therof; he hastede hym self and alle his oste towarde the towne
of Glouceter, but he enteryd noȝt into the towne, but held forthe
his wey to the towne of Teukesbury, and ther he made a felde
noȝt ferre from the ryver of Saverne; and Kynge Edwarde and
his oste came uppone hym, the saturday the fourth day of Maij,
the yere aforeseide of oure Lorde a Mˡ. cccclxxj., and the xj yere
of Kynge Edwarde. And Edmunde Duke of Somersett, and Sere
Hugh Curteneye, went oute of the felde, by the whiche the felde
was broken; and the moste parte of the peple fledde awaye from
the Prynce, by the whiche the feld was loste in hire party.
And ther was slayne in the felde, Prynce Edward, whiche cryede
for socoure to his brother-in-lawe the Duke of Clarence. Also
ther was slayne, Curteney the Erle of Devynschyre, the Lorde
Jhon of Somersett, the Lorde Wenloke, Sere Edmunde Hampden,
Sere Robart Whytyngham, Sere William Vaus, Sere Nicholas
Hervy, Sere Jhon Delvis, Sere William Feldynge, Sere Thomas
Fiztharry, Sere Jhon Leukenore, knyghtes; and these were taken
and behedede afterwarde, where the Kynge hade pardoned them
in the abbey cherche of Teukesbury, by a prest that turnyd oute
at his messe and the sacrament in his handys, whanne Kynge
Edwarde came with his swerde into the chirche, requyrede hyme
by the vertu of the sacrament that he schulde pardone alle tho
whos names here folowe; the Duke of Somersett, the Lorde of
Seynt Jhones, Sere Humfrey Audeley, Sere Gervis of Clyftone,
Sere William Gremyby, Sere William Cary, Sere Thomas Tresham, Sere William Newbrugh, knyghtes, Herry Tresham, Walter
Curtenay, Jhon Florey, Lowes Myles, Robart Jacksone, James
Gowere, James Delvis, sonne and heire to Sere Jhon Delvis;

whiche, uppone trust of the Kynges pardone yevene in the same chirche the saturday, abode ther stille, where thei myght have gone and savyd ther lyves; whiche one monday aftere were behedede, no3twhitstondynge the Kynges pardone. And afterward these ladyes were takene,—Quene Margaret, Prynce Edwardes wyf, the secunde dowghtere of the Erle of Warwykes, the Countasse of Devynschire, Dame Kateryne Vaus. And these were taken, and no3t slayne; Sere Jhon Fortescu, Sere Jhon Sentlow, Sire Herry Roos, Thomas Ormonde, Doctour Makerell, Edward Fulforde, Jhon Parkere, Jhon Bassett, Jhon Wallys, Jhon Thromere Throgmertone, and dyverse other men. And there was takene grete good, and many good horse that were brought frome beyond the see.

And in the same tyme that the batelle of Teukesbury was, Sere Watere Wrotty[s]le and Geffrei Gate, knygtes of the Erle of Warwykes, were governers of the towne of Caleys, dide sende Sere George Broke knyghte oute of Caleys, with ccc. of soudyours unto Thomas Bastarde Fakynebrygge, that was one the see with the Erle of Warwykes navy, that he schulde the navy save, and goo into Kent, and to reyse alle Kent, to that entente to take Kynge Herry oute of the toure and distroye Kyng Edwarde, yf he myghte; whiche Bastarde came into Kent, to Caunturbury, and he, withe helpe of other gentylmenne, thei reysed up alle Kent, and came to Londone the v. day of Maij the yere aforeseide. But thenne the Lorde Scales, that Kynge Edwarde hade lefte to kepe the cyte, with the Meyre and Aldermen, wulde no3t suffre the seid Bastarde to come into the cite; for thei had understondynge that Prince Edwarde was dede, and alle his hoste discomfytede: wherefor the Bastarde loosede his gonnes into the citee, and brent at Algate and at Londone brygge; for the whiche brynnynge, the comons of Londone where sore wrothe, and gretely mevyd ayens them: for and thei had no3t brent, the comons of the cyte wulde have leett them in, magre of the Lorde Scales hede, the Mayre and alle his brethyr. Wherefor the Bastarde and alle his hoste went overe at Kyngstone Brygge, x. myle westwarde, and hade purposed to have distruyt Kynge Edwarde, or to have dryve hym oute of the londe. And if the Bastarde hade holde forthe his way, Kynge Edwarde be possibilyte coude noȝt be powere haf recisted the Bastarde; for the Bastarde hade moo then xx. ꝳᶫ. goode men welle harnessede, and evere as he went the peple felle to hym. The Lorde Scales, and dyverse othere of Kynge Edwardes counselle that were in Londone, sawe that the Bastarde and his oste went westwarde, and that it schuld be a grettere juperdy to Kynge Edwarde thenne was Barnet felde or Teukesbury felde, (in so moche when the felde of Teukesbury was done, his oste was departede from;) wherefor thei promysed to the Bastarde, and to dyverse other that were aboute hym, and in especyalle to one Nicholas Fauntt, Meyre of Caunterbury, that he schulde entret hym to turne homwarde ageyn. And for as myche as fayre wordes and promyses makes fooles fayne, the Bastarde commaundede alle his oste to turne to Blakhethe ageyn; whiche was distruccion of hyme self and many othere; for anone after, by the Duke of Gloucetre in Yorkeschyre, the seide Bastarde was behedede, noȝtwithstondynge he hade a chartere of pardone; and Nicholas Fauntt was afterward hangede, drawene, and quarterede in Caunterbury. And whene the Bastarde and alle his oste were come to the Blakheth ageyne, in the next mornynge he withe the soudyours and schypmen of Caleis, to the nombre of vj. c. horsemen, stole awaye frome the oste and roode to Rouchester, and frome thens to Sandwyche, where the Bastard abode the Kynges comynge, and the soudyours saylede overe see to Caleys. And whenne the oste understode that ther Capteyne was stole from them, thei kepte them togedere alle a day and a nyght, and thanne every manne departede to his owne howse. And when Kynge Edward herde thereof, he was gladde, &c.

Here is to knowe that Kynge Edwarde made oute commyssyons to many schyres of Englonde; whiche in a x. dayes ther came to hym, where he was, to the nowmbre of xxx. ꝳᶫ., and came

withe the Kynge to Londone, and ther he was worschipfully receyvid. And the same nyghte that Kynge Edwarde came to Londone, Kynge Herry, beynge inwarde in presone in the Toure of
Londone, was putt to dethe, the xxj. day of Maij, on a tywesday
nyght, betwyx xj. and xij. of the cloke, beynge thenne at the Toure
the Duke of Gloucetre, brothere to Kynge Edwarde, and many
other; and one the morwe he was chestyde and brought to Paulys,
and his face was opyne that every manne myghte see hyme; and
in hys lyinge he bledde one the pament ther; and afterward at
the Blake Fryres was broughte, and ther he blede new and fresche;
and from thens he was caryed to Chyrchesey abbey in a bote, and
buryed there in oure Lady chapelle. On the morwe that the
Kynge was come to Londone, for the goode servyse that Londone
hade done to hym, he made knyghtes of the Aldermenne, Sere
Jhon Stokstone, Sire Rauf Verney, Sere Richard Lee, Sere Jhon
Yonge, Sere William Tayliour, Sere George Irlande, Sere Jhon
Stokere, Sere Mathew Philyppe, Sere William Hamptone, Sere
Thomas Stalbroke, Sere Jhon Crosby, Sere Thomas Urswike,
Recordere of Londone. And after that, the Kynge and alle his
oste roode into Kent to Caunterbury, where many of the countre
that where at Blakhethe withe the Bastarde, were arestede and
brought befor hym; and ther was hangyd, drawene, and quarteryd,
one Fauntt of Caunterbury, that was lovynge to the Erle of
Warwyke; whyche entreytede the Bastarde for to departe frome
his oste; and many dyverse menne of the cuntre were hanged
and put to dethe. Aftere that, the Kynge roode unto Sanwyche,
and beside alle the Erle of Warwykes navy there, that the
Bastarde hade reule of, and toke the Bastard withe hyme, and
returned ageyne to Londone. And immediatly after that was the
Lorde Denham and Sere Jhon Fog and dyverse othere made com-
myssioners, that satt uppone alle Kent, Sussex, and Esex, that
were at the Blakhethe, and uppone many othere that were noȝt
there; for some manne payed cc. marke, some a c. pownde, and some

more and some lesse, so that it coste the porest manne vij. s. whiche was noʒt worthe so myche, but was fayne to selle suche clothinge as thei hade, and borowede the remanent, and laborede for it aftyrwarde; and so the Kynge hade out of Kent myche goode and lytelle luff. Lo, what myschef groys after insurreccion! &c. ɩ

And in [the] same xj. yere of the Kynge, in the begynnynge of of Januarij, there apperyd the moste mervelous blasynge sterre that hade bene seyne. It aroose in the southe este, at ij. of the cloke at mydnyghte, and so contynuede a xij. nyghtes; and it arose ester and ester, tille it aroose fulle este; and rather, and rather; and so whenne it roose playne est, it rose at x. of cloke in the nyght, and kept his cours flamynge westwarde overe Englonde; and it hade a white flaume of fyre fervently brennynge, and it flammede endlonges fro the est to the weste, and noʒt upryght, and a grete hole therin, whereof the flawme came oute of. And aftyre a vj. or vij. dayes, it aroose north-est, and so bakkere and bakkere; and so enduryd a xiiij. nyghtes, fulle lytelle chaungynge, goynge from the north-este to the weste, and some tyme it wulde seme aquenchede oute, and sodanly it brent fervently ageyne. And thenne it was at one tyme playne northe, and thenne it compassede rounde aboute the lodesterre, for in the evynynge the blase went ageyns the southe, and in the mornynge playne northe, and thenne afterwarde west, and so more west, flaumyng up ryghte; and so the sterre contynuede iiij. wekys, tylle the xx. day of Feveryere; and whenne it appered yest in the fyrmament, thenne it lasted alle the nyghte, somewhat discendyng withe a grettere smoke one the heyre. And some menne seyde that the blassynges of the seide sterre was of a myle length. And a xij. dayes afore the vanyschynge therof, it appereryd in the evynynge, and was downe anone within two oures, and evyr of a colour pale stedfast; and it kept his course rysynge west in the northe, and so every nyght, it apperide lasse and lasse tylle it was as lytelle as a hesylle styke; and so at the laste it waneschede away the xx. day of Februarij. And some menne saide that this sterre was seene ij. or iij. oures afore the sunne rysynge in Decembre, iiij. days before Crystynmasse, in the south-west; so by that reasoune it compassed rounde abowte alle the erthe, alle way chaungynge his cours, as is afore reherside.

: And in the xij. yere of Kynge Edwarde, he lete calle a parleament to be holdene at Westmynstere, the qwhiche beganne the viij. day after Michaelmasse the same yere; in qwiche parleament was a generalle resumpcion of alle lordschippes, tenamentes, and other possesions and feys grawntede be the Kynge, frome the fyrst day of his regne unto the day aforeseid. Also ther was grauntyde, in the same parleamente, that the x. parte of every mannys good, londes, tenamentes, rentys, and feys, thrugheoute alle Englonde, the valowe therof as for a yere; and also a hole quynsyme amonge the comons, to be reysede, of goodes and catelle; and also lj. Ml. vij. c. li. of money to be raysed, of alle mennys londes, goodes, and other possessions within the reame of Englonde. Also ther was grawntede to the Kynge by the spiritualte, in a convocacion two dymes and prestes markes thurghtoute alle Englonde: whiche alle was grauntede by the desyre of the Kyng, for he seide he wuld overe see and conquere his right and title in Fraunce, Normandy, Gascoyne, and Guyane.

Also in xiij. yere of Kynge Edwarde, ther was a gret hote somere, bothe for manne and beste; by the whiche ther was gret dethe of menne and women, that in feld in harvist tyme men fylle downe sodanly, and unyversalle feveres, axes, and the blody flyx, in dyverse places of Englonde. And also the hete was so grete, that it brent awey whete and alle other greynis and gresse, in southe partyes of the worlde, in Spayne, Portyngale, Granade, and othere, &c. that a bowsshelle of whete was worthe xx. s; and menne were fayne in that cuntre to yeve away there childeryne for to fynde them. But, blessede be Almyghty God, no suche derthe was noȝt in Englonde, ne in Fraunce.

Also in the same yere Womere watere ranne hugely, withe suche abundaunce of watere, that nevyr manne sawe it renne so moche afore this tyme. Womere is callede the woo watere: for Englyschmen, whenne thei dyd fyrst inhabyde this lond, also sone as thei see this watere renne, thei knewe wele it was a tokene of derthe, or of pestylence, or of grete batayle; wherefor thei callede it *Womere;* (for *we* as in Englysche tonge woo, and *mere* is called watere, whiche signyfieth woo-watere;) for alle that tyme thei sawe it renne, thei knewe welle that woo was comynge to Englonde. And this Wemere is vij. myle frome Sent Albons, at a place callede Markayate; and this Wemere ranne at every felde afore specifyede, and nevere so hugely as it dyd this yere, and ranne stylle to the xiij. day of June next yere folowynge. Also ther has ronne dyverse suche other wateres, that betokenethe lykewyse; one at Lavesham in Kent, and another byside Canturbury called Naylborne, and another at Croydone in Suthsex, and another vij. myle a this syde the castelle of Dodley, in the place called Hungerevale; that whenne it betokenethe batayle it rennys foule and trouble watere; and whenne betokenythe derthe or pestylence, it rennyth as clere as any watere, but this yere it ranne ryght trouble and foule watere, &c. Also ther is a pytte in Kent, in Langley Parke: ayens any batayle he wille be drye, and it rayne nevere so myche; and if ther be no batayle towarde, he wille be fulle of watere, be it nevyre so drye a wethyre; and this yere he is drye, &c. Also this same yere, ther was a voyce cryenge in the heyre, betwyx Laicetere and Bambury, uppon Dunmothe, and in dyverse othere places, herde a long tyme cryinge, "Bowes! Bowes!" whiche was herde of xl. menne; and some menne saw that he that cryed soo was a hedles manne; and many other dyverse tokenes have be schewede in Englonde this yere, for amendynge of mennys lyvynge.

· Also this yere, or a lytelle before, George the Archebysshoppe of Yorke, and brother to the Erle of Warwyke, was withe Kynge Edwarde at Wynsoure, and huntede, and hade there ryghte good chere, and supposid he hade stonde in grete favour with the Kynge: for the

Kynge seid to the sayde Archebyschope that he wuld come for to hunte and disporte withe hyme in his manere at Moore; whereof he was ryghte glade, and toke his leve and went home to make purvyaunce therfore; and fett oute of Londone, and dyverse other places, alle his plate and othere stuffe that he hade hyde after Barnet felde and Teukysbury feld; and also borowede more stuff of other menne, and purveyde for the Kynge for two or iij. dayes for mete and drynke and logynge, and arayed as rychely and as plesauntly as he coude. And the day afore the Kynge schulde have comyne to the Archebyssshoppe, to the seid manere of Moore, whiche the saide Archebisshoppe hade purchasshed and byllede it ryghte comodiusly and plesauntly, the Kynge send a gentylman to the seide Archebisshoppe, and commaundyd him to come to Wyndsoure to hyme; and asone as he came he was arested and apeched of hye treysone, that he schuld helpe the Erle of Oxenforde; and anone ryght he was put to warde. And forthe-withe Sere William of Parre, knyghte, and Thomas Vaghan, squyre, withe othere many dyverse gentilmenne and yomen, were sent to the seide manere of Moore; and ther by the Kynges comawnde-ment seysede the seid manere into the Kynges handes, and alle the good that was therin, whiche was worthe xx. m^l. ^{li}. or more, and alle other lordschippes and landes that the seid bysshoppe hade wíthein Englonde, and alle his stuff and rychesse wíthein alle his lordschippes; and sent the same bisschoppe overe the sec to Caleis, and from thens to the castelle of Hammys, and ther he was kepte presonere many a day; and the Kynge alle that seasone toke the prophete of the Archebysshopperyche, &c. And anone after the Kynge brake the seyd Archebysschoppes mytere, in the whiche were fulle many ryche stones and preciouse, and made therof a croune for hyme self. And alle his other juels, plate, and stuff, the Kynge gaff it to his eldest sonne and heyre Prynce Edward: for the sayd Archebisshoppe hade be Chaun-selere of Englond many dayes, and he and his brotheres hade the reule of the lande, and hade gaderyde grete rychesse many yeres, whiche in one day was lost; and alle be the hye jugement of ryghtwisnes (as many manne seide be hym) for his grete cove-tousenes, and had no pyte of Kynge Harry menne, and was cause of many mannys undoynge for Kynge Edwardys sake, if he myghte gete any good by hym. Wherefore *suche goodes as were gaderide with synne, were loste with sorwe.* And also menne supposid for cause he was duble to Kynge Herry, and kepte hym in Londone, where he wulde a be at Westmynstere, he hade a lettere send frome Kynge Edward to kepe hym oute of sanctuary, and he hade his charture send hym; where he had be a trewe manne to Kynge Herry, as the comons of Londone were, Kynge Edward hade not comene into Londone afore Barnet felde, &c.

Also in the xiij. yere of [the] regne of Kynge Edwarde, Sere Jhon Veere, Erle of Oxenforde, that withdrewe hym frome Barnet felde, and rode into Scottlonde, and frome thens into Fraunce asailed, and ther he was worschipfully received. And in the same yere he was in the see withe certeyne schippes, and gate grete good and rychesse, and afterewarde came into westecountre, and, with a sotule poynte of werre, gate and enteryd Seynt Michaels Mount in Cornwayle, a stronge place and a mygty, and can no3t be geett yf it be wele vytaled withe a fewe menne to kepe hit; for xxti. menne may kepe it ageyne alle the world. So the seyde Erle, withe xxti. score menne save iij, the last day of Septembre the yere afore seyd, enteryd fyrst into [the] seyd mount, and he and his menne came doune into cuntre of Cornwale, and hade riyhte good chere of the comons, &c. The Kynge and his counselle sawe that therof myche harme myght growe, &c.; comawndyd Bodrygan, scheff reulere of Cornwayle, to besege the seid mount. And so he dyd; and every day the Erle of Oxenfordes menne came doune undere trewis, spake with Bodrynghan and his menne; and at the laste the seid Erle lacked vytayle, and the seyde Bodrygan suffryd hyme to be vytailed; and anone the Kynge was put in knowlache therof; wherefor the

seide Bodrygan was discharged, and Richard Fortescu, squyere for
the body, by auctoryte of the Kynge, toke uppone honde to lay
sege to the forseide mount, &c. And so gret dyversione roose
betwyx Bodrygan and Fortescu, whiche Fortescu was schreve of
Cornwayle, &c.; and the seide Fortescu leyed sege, &c. the xx. xiij^{ti}.
day of Decembre the yere aforseide; and for the most party
every day eche of theme faughte withe othere, and the seide
Erles menne kylled dyverse of Fortescu menne; and som tyme
whenne thei hade welle y-foughte, thei wulde take a trewis for one
day and a night, and some tyme for two or thre dayes, &c. In the
whiche trewes eche one of them spake and comaunde with other.
The Kynge and his counselle sent unto dyverse that were with
the Erle of Oxenforde prevely there pardones, and promysede to
them grete yeftes and landes and goodes, by the whiche dyverse
of them were turned to the Kynge ayens the Erle; and so in
conclusione the Erle hade no3t passynge ane viij. or ix. menne
that wolde holde withe hym; the whiche was the undoynge of
the Erle. For ther is proverbe and a seyenge, that *a castelle
that spekythe, and a womane that wille here, thei wille be gotene
bothe :* for menne that bene in a castelle of warr, that wille speke
and entrete withe ther enemyes, the conclusione therof [is] the
losynge of the castelle ; and a womanne that wille here foly spokyne
unto hyre, if sche assent no3t at one tyme, sche wille at another.
And so this proverbe was prevede trewe by the seide Erle of Oxenforde, whiche was fayne to yelde up the seyde mount, and put hyme
in the Kynges grace; if he hade no3t do so, his owne menne wulde
have brought hym oute. And so Fortescu enterd into the seyd
mount, the xv. day of Februarij. the yere afore sayde, in the whiche
was vytayle enogh tylle midsomere aftere. And so was the Erle
aforseyd, the Lorde Bemonde, two brotheres of the seide Erles,
and Thomas Clyfforde, brought as a presonere to the Kynge;
and alle was donne by ther oun εfoly, &c.

NOTES.

P. 1, *l.* 1.—The Warkworth Chronicle, in Bernard's Catalogue of the Peterhouse manuscripts, taken from James's Eclogæ, is numbered—230. It may be as well to observe that John Bagford mentions a contemporary Chronicle in English MS. of the events of. the commencement of Edward's reign, in MS. Tann. Bodl. 453.

—— *l.* 3.—*At the coronacyone.* King Edward was crowned in Westminster Abbey, on the 29th of June 1461. Warkworth's first passage is both imperfect and incorrect, and would form a very bad specimen of the value of the subsequent portions of his narrative ; yet we find it transferred to the Chronicle of Stowe. It must, however, be regarded rather as a memorandum of the various creations to the peerage made during Edward's reign, than as a part of the chronicle. Not even the third peerage mentioned, the Earldom of Northumberland, was conferred at the Coronation, but by patent dated 27 May 1464 : and the only two Earldoms bestowed in Edward's first year (and probably at the Coronation) were, the Earldom of Essex, conferred on Henry Viscount Bourchier, Earl of Eu in Normandy, who had married the King's aunt, the Princess Isabel of York ; and the Earldom of Kent, conferred on William Neville, Lord Fauconberg, one of King Edward's generals at Towton. The former creaion is mentioned by Warkworth lower down in his list ; the latter is omitted altogether.—J. G. N.

—— *l.* 6.—*The Lord Montagu.* " And then Kyng Edward, concidering the great feate doon by the said Lord Montagu, made hym Erle of Northumberlond ; and in July next folowyng th'Erle of Warwyk, with th'ayde of the said Erle of Northumberland, gate agayn the castell of Bamborugh, wheryn was taken Sir Raaf Gray, which said Ser Raaf was after behedid and quartred at York. Also, in this yere, the first day of May, the Kyng wedded Dame Elizabeth Gray, late wif unto the lord Gray of Groby, and doughter to the Lord Ryvers."—*The London Chronicle*, MS. Cotton. Vitell. A. xvi. fol. 126, r°. The MS. of the London Chronicle, from which Sir Harris Nicolas printed his edition, does not contain this passage. It is almost unnecessary to remark the chronological incorrectness of the above, but it serves to show how carelessly these slight Chronicles were compiled. Cf. MS. Add. Mus. Brit. 6113, fol. 192, r°. and MS. Cotton. Otho, B. xiv. fol. 221, r°.

P. 1, *l.* 9.—*Lord Erle of Pembroke.* William Lord Herbert of Chepstow, the first of the long line of Herbert Earls of Pembroke, was so created the 27th May 1468. His decapitation by the Duke of Clarence at Northampton in 1469, is noticed by Warkworth in p. 7.—J. G. N.

—— *l.* 10.—*Erle of Devynschire.* Humphery Stafford, created Baron Stafford of Southwick by patent 24th April 1464, was advanced to the Earldom of Devon 7th May 1469; but beheaded by the commons at Bridgwater before the close of the same year, as related by Warkworth, *ubi supra.*—J. G. N.

—— *l.* 12.—*Erle of Wyltschyre.* John Stafford, created Earl of Wiltshire, 5th Jan. 1470; he died in 1473.—J. G. N.

The Lorde Gray Ruffyne, Erle of Kent. The Earl of Kent, of the family of Neville, died without male issue, a few months after his elevation to that dignity; and it was conferred on the 30th May 1465, on Edmund Lord Grey de Ruthyn, on occasion of the Queen's coronation. He was cousin-german to Sir John Grey, of Groby, the Queen's first husband. On the same occasion the Queen's son Sir Thomas Grey was created Marquess of Dorset; her father Richard Wydevile lord Ryvers was advanced to the dignity of Earl Ryvers; and her brother Anthony married to the heiress of Scales, in whose right he was summoned to Parliament as a Baron.—J. G. N.

Ibid.—*Sere Thomas Blount.* This should be *Walter*, created Lord Montjoy 20th June 1465; he died in 1474.—J. G. N.

P. 1, l. 13.—Sere Jhon Hawarde, Lord Hawarde. This peerage dates its origin, by writ of summons to Parliament, during the short restoration of Henry VI. in 1470, a circumstance more remarkable as "evidence exists that he did not attach himself to the interest of that Prince, being constitued by Edward, in the same year, commander of his fleet." See Sir Harris Nicolas's memoir of this distinguished person (afterwards the first Duke of Norfolk) in Cartwright's History of the Rape of Bramber, p. 189.—J. G. N.

—— *l. 18.—He ordeyned a parleament.* This was in November.

—— *l. 19.—At whiche were atteynted Kynge Henry.* The act for the attainder of Henry is not printed in the authentic edition of the Statutes of the Realm, published by the Commissioners for the Public Records, but occurs on the Rolls of Parliament, vol. v. pp. 476—82. Cf. MS. Ashm. 21, and 862, xxxv; *Cotton's Abridgment,* pp. 670—1 ; *Fœdera,* xi. 709. " Ubi indutati et atteyntati sunt Henricus, vocatus nuper Rex Anglie, cum Margareta* consore sua, duces et Somerset et Excetre, cum aliis militibus et nobilibus ad numerum quasi centum personarum." MS. Arundel, Coll. Arm. 5, fol. 169, r⁰. Cf. *W. Wyrcestre Annales,* pp. 490—2.

P. 2, l. 3.—New Fraunschesses. Cf. MS. Bib. Cantuar. 51.

—— *l. 6.—Also Quene Margrett.* This was in the year 1462. Towards the end of the year Edward appears to have made a tour to the West of England, perhaps for the purpose of seeing how the country was disposed towards him :—" Deinde Rex Edwardus, Cantuariam peregre profectus, partes meridionales pertransiit, ubi Willielmum Episcopum Wintonie de manibus querentium animam ejus eripuit, insectatores suos graviter redarguit, et eorum capitaneos carcerali custodi emancipavit. Bristollie apperians, a civibus ejus cum max-

---

* I find, however, in the Pipe Roll of 1 Edw. IV. an entry of £21. 13s. for property at Bristol to " Margareta nuper dicta Regina Angliæ," granted to her by Edward ; this property, it appears, formerly belonged to Queen Johanna, and " per dominum Regem nunc concess' in partem recompensacionis."

imo gaudio honoratissimè receptus est."—MS. Arundel, Coll. Arm.
5, fol. 169, r°.   This Chronicle in the College of Arms was first used,
as far as I know, for an historical purpose, in a MS. note in a copy
of Carte's History of England in the Bodleian Library, where it is
referred to on the important testimony of the death of Henry VI.
Mr. Black quotes it in the *Excerpta Historica*, but its value does not
appear to be fully appreciated by that author; it is the diary of a
contemporary writer on the side of the House of York, and extends
to the execution of the Bastard of Fauconberg, and Edward's cele-
bration of the feast of Pentecost which took place immediately
afterwards.

The following very curious account of the pageant which received
Edward at Bristol is from a MS. in Lambeth Palace, N°. 306, fol.
132, r°.   I am indebted for it to the Rev. S. R. Maitland, F.R.S.,
Librarian to the Archbishop of Canterbury, who had the extreme
kindness, at my request, to send me a transcript.

" The receyvyng of Kyng Edward the iiij[th]*. at Brystowe.*

" First, at the comyng inne atte temple gate, there stode Wylliam
Conquerour, with iij. lordis, and these were his wordis :—

> ' Wellcome Edwarde ! oure son of high degre ;
> Many yeeris hast thou lakkyd owte of this londe—
> I am thy forefader, Wylliam of Normandye,
> To see thy welefare here through Goddys sond.'

" Over the same gate stondyng a greet Gyant delyveryng the keyes.

" The Receyvyng atte Temple Crosse next following ;—

" There was Seynt George on horsbakke, uppon a tent, fyghtyng
with a dragon ; and the Kyng and the Quene on hygh in a castell,
and his doughter benethe with a lambe ; and atte the sleying of the
dragon ther was a greet melody of aungellys."

Sir Bawdan (or Baldwin) Fulford was brought before the King, and beheaded at this place on the ninth of September; his head was placed upon Castle Gate.—Rot. C. 8. Mus. Brit.

P. 2, l. 7.—And other lordes. Among them was Thomas Lord Roos. *Paston Correspondence,* vol. I. p. 219.

—— *l. 7-8.—Certeyne castelles in Northumberlond.* See two contemporary accounts of the sieges of these castles, edited by Mr. Black, in the *Excerpta Historica,* p. 365. Cf. *W. Wyrcestre,* p. 493—449.

—— *l. 16.—Sere Peris le Brasylle.* See a curious document printed by Sir Henry Ellis, from Cart. Antiq. Cotton. XVII. 10. in the second series of his collection of Original Letters, vol. I. p. 131.

P. 3, l. 7.—Excepte a castelle in Northe Wales called Harlake. I cannot resist the temptation of taking the following lines from the poems of Lewis Glyn Cothi, relative to the future siege of Harlech castle—

> " Doves â'i wyr, divasw wedd,
> Dareni daiar Wynedd ;
> Jarll, ond ev a'r llu, nid â
> Ar wddv Eryri Wyddva.
> Dau er ei chael dri a chwech,—
> Un dân harddlun yw Harddlech.
> Tynu â gwyr tònau gwin
> Peiriannus, val mab brenin.
> Uchel ewri a *chlariwns,*
> A tharvu gwyr â thwrv *gwns ;*
> Saethu 'mhob parth saith mil pen,
> A'u bwa o bob ywen :
> Clod wellwell, cludaw allan
> Goed mawr a fagodau mân ;
> O wartha 'r rhai'n, hyd yr hwyr,
> Arvogion a'u rhyvagwyr.
> Trwy'r tair gwart Herbart hirborth
> Ty'nu'r pen capten i'r porth.
> Ennillodd, eu ewyllys,
> Y brenin lech Bronwen Lys.
>   *Hywel Davydd ab Jevan ab Rhys."*

As no translation is added in the published works of Glyn Cothi, it may be as well to give one here;—

> " He tamed, in no trifling manner,
> The lofty heights of Gwyneth ;*
> No earl, save him and his followers, could ever mount
> Upon the neck of Snowdon, the Alpine of Eryri.†
> There would climb up, to gain the ascent,
> Now three,—now six men, all at once ;
> One beautifully formed fiery blaze is Harddlech ! ‡
> Men drawing from men waves of wine,— §
> Loud the shouting—loud the blasts of clarions ;
> Scattering of men, thundering of guns ;
> Arrows flying in every quarter from seven thousand men,
> Using bows made of the yew.
> Bravo ! bravo ! they bring out large trees and faggots ;
> They pile them up, and, behind the pile,
> Armed men are placed to continue there 'til night.
> Then Herbert, through the three wards,
> Brings forth the head captain in the porch.
> Thus King Edward, as it were, with one volition,
> Gained possession of Bronwen's Court.''||

This place was possessed in 1468 by Dafydd ap Jeuan ap Einion,— a strong friend of the house of Lancaster, distinguished for his valour and great stature. He was besieged here by William Herbert, Earl of Pembroke, after a march through the heart of our Alps, attended with incredible difficulties ; for in some parts, the soldiers were obliged to climb ; in others, to precipitate themselves down the rocks ; and, at length, invested a place till that time deemed impregnable.

* North Wales.   † The mountains surrounding Snowdon.
‡ This couplet is metaphorical of the rapidity of Herbert's motions.
§ i. e. streams of blood.
|| The castle was anciently called Twr Bronwen, after Bronwen, daughter of Llyr (King Lear), and aunt to the great Caractacus. See *The Cambro-Briton*, ii. 71. She is the subject of an old Welsh Romance.

The Earl committed the care of the siege to Sir Richard, a hero equal in size to the British commandant. Sir Richard sent a summons of surrender, but Dafydd stoutly answered that he had kept a castle in France so long, that he made all the old women in Wales talk of him; and that he would keep this so long, that all the old women in France should also talk of him. He at last surrendered, and Herbert had a hard struggle with Edward's barbarous policy to save the noble defender's life.—*Pennant's Tour in Wales*, vol. II. p. 121-2. Margaret of Anjou found refuge in this Castle after the unfortunate battle of Northampton; and it has been conjectured that the song of " Farwel iti Peggy Ban" was composed on the occasion of her quitting it. On the peculiar advantages of the position of this castle, see *The Cambrian Traveller's Guide*, p. 574.

P. 3, *l.* 15-6.—*An hole quinzisme and disme.* See *Rot. Parl. V.* 497. This parliament met on the 29th of April, and continued to the following year.

—— *l.* 16.—*Whereof the peple grocehede sore.* The taxes which Edward appears to have levied were most onerous on the people, and partly served to pay for his extravagant luxury, which he seems to have carried to the extreme.—*Cambrian Register,* I. 78.

—— *l.* 17-8.—*The Erle of Warwyke was sent into Fraunce.* Gagvin, in his Chronicon Franciæ, informs us that the Earl was received by the King Louis XI. at Rouen with great pomp; had secret conferences with him for twelve days consecutively; and was loaded with presents when he took his departure. It is curious to observe that the author of the fragment printed by Hearne refers to a French writer on this portion of his history.

—— *l.* 21.—*The Kynge was wedded to Elizabethe Gray.* See a most quaint narrative of this marriage in William Habington's *Historie of Edward the Fourth*, fol. 1640, pp. 33—35. I find it stated in one place (MS. Harl. 2408.) that Edward's mother attempted to hinder the marriage, by causing " another contract to be alleadged made by him with the Lady Elizabeth Lucy, on whom he had begot a child befor." She seems, indeed, to have been most hostile to this imprudent and unpopular connexion :—

> " Married a woman? married indeed!
> Here is a marriage that befits a king!
> It is no marvaile it was done in hast:
> Here is a bridall, and with hell to boote,
> You have made worke."
> *Heywood's First Part of Edward IV.* Sig. A. ij.

The author of Hearne's fragment, however, speaks in praise of the marriage,—" Howbeit that lewde felow that drew thois last brent cronicles, abusid himsel gretely in his disordrid wri3ting for lakke of knowlege." (P. 293.)

P. 3, l. 23.—Slayne at Yorke felde. Sir John Grey was slain at the second battle of St. Alban's, fought on the 17th Feb. 1460–1.—J. G. N.

——— *l. 30.—The Bysshope of Excetre.* George Neville, made Chancellor the 25th July 1460. He was translated to the archbishopric of York, 17th June 1465.—J. G. N.

——— *l. 31.—The Bysshope of Bath.* Robert Stillington. He did not receive the seal until the 8th June 1468, previously to which Robert Kirkham had been Keeper.—J. G. N.

P. 4, l. 2.—Kyng Edwarde dide that he myght to feble the Erles powerc. We have, however, in an act passed subsequently to this period, an especial clause that the same act " be not prejudiciall or hurtyng unto Richard Neville, Erle of Warrewyk."—*Rot. Parl.* 4 *Edw. IV.*

——— *l. 8.—Godred a grete peple of the northe contre.* The following very curious document is from a MS. in the College of Arms (L. 9):—

" *Anno Edwaidi quarti quarto et mensis Maij die xxvij. scilicet in die san[c]te Trinitatis.*

" The Kyng lay in the Palois of York, and kept his astate solemply; and tho there create he Sir John Nevelle, Lord Mowntage, Erle of Northumberland. And than my lorde of Warrewike toke upon hym the jorney, by the Kynges commandement and auctoritee, to resiste the Rebellions of the Northe, acompanyed with hym my sayde Lorde of Northumberland his brother.

" Item, the xxiij^{ti}. day of Juyne, my saide Lorde of Warrewike, with the puissaunce, cam before the castelle of Alwike, and ad it delivered by appointement; And also the castell of Dunstanboroughe, where that my said Lord kept the feest of Saint Johñ Baptist.

" Item, my said Lorde of Warrewike, and his broder Erle of Northumberland, the xxv. day of Juyn, leyede siege unto the Castelle of Bamburghe, there within being Sir Rauf Grey, with suche power as attendid for to keepe the said castelle ayen the power of the Kinges and my said Lord, as it apperith by the heroudes reporte, by the whiche my Lord sent to charge them to delyvere it under this forme, as ensewithe; Chester, the Kinges heroude, and Warrewike the heroude, had this commaundement, as foloweth,—to say unto Sir Rauf Gray, and to other that kept his Rebelliouse oppynyon, that they shule delivere that place contynent aftyr that summacion, and every man for the tyme being disposed to receyve the Kynges grace, my said Lord of Warrewike, the Kinges lieutenant, and my Lord of Northumbreland, Wardeyn of themarches, grauntith the Kyng['s] grace and pardon, body, lyvelodes, reservyng ij. persounes, is understoude, Sir Humfrey Neville and Sir Rauf Grey, thoo tweyn to be oute of the Kinges grace, without any redempcion. Than the answere of Sir Rauf Grey followithe unto the said heroudes, he clerely determynyng withinne hymself to liffe or to dye within the said place; the heroudes, according to my Lordes commandement, charged hym with all inconveniences that by possible myght fall in offence ayenst Allemyghty God, and sheding of bloode; the heroude saying in this wise, ' My Lordes ensurithe yow, upon their honour, to susteyne siege before yowe these vij. yeres, or elles to wynne yowe.'

" Item, my sayde Lorde Lieutenant, and my Lord Wardeyn, hath yeven us ferther comaundement to say unto yowe, if ye deliver not this Juelle, the whiche the king our most dradde soverain Lord hath so gretly in favour, seing it marcheth so nygh hys awncient enemyes of Scotland, he specially desirethe to have it, hoole, unbroken, with ordennaunce; if ye suffre any greet gunne laide unto the wal, and be

shote and prejudice the wal, it shall cost yowe the Chiftens hede;
and so proceding for every gunne shet, to the leest hede of any per-
soune within the said place. Than the saide Sir Rauf Grey deperted
from the saide heroud, ant put hym in devoir to make deffence.

" And than my Lorde lieutenant had ordennede alle the Kinges
greet gonnes that where charged at oons to shute unto the said Castelle, Newe-Castel the Kinges greet gonne, and London the second
gonne of irne; the whiche betyde the place, that stones of the
walles flewe unto the see; Dysyon, a brasin gonne of the Kinges,
smote thouroughe Sir Rauf Grey's chamber oftentymes; Edward
and Richard Bombartell, and other of the Kinges ordennaunce, so
occupied by the ordonnaunce of my said Lord, with men of armes
and archirs, wonne the castelle of Bamburg with asawte, mawgrey
Sir Rauf Grey, and tooke hym, and brought hym to the Kynge to
Doncastre, and there was he execut in this fourme as followith. My
lorde Erle of Worcestre, Connestable of Englond, sitting in jugement, told hym jugement, and remambrid hym, saying unto hym;
" Sir Rauf Grey, thou hast take the ordir of Knyghthode of the
Batthe, and any soe taking that ordir ought to kepe his faithe the
whiche he makes; therfor remembre the[e] the lawe! wilt thou shall
procede to jugement? thees maters shewith so evidently agayn the,
that they nedithe not to examyn the of them, by certein persounes of
the Kinges true subgettes, the whiche thou hast wounded, and shewithe
here that thou canst not deny this; thou hast drawen the with force
of armes unto the Kyng oure most natural soverain Lorde, the whiche
tho wotest wele yave unto the suche trust, and in suche wise mynys-
tred his grace unto the, that thou haddist his castels in the Northe
partie to kepe; thou hast betraied Sir John Asteley Knyght, and
brother of the gartier, the whiche remaignethe in the hand of the
Kynges oure soverain Lord enemyes in Fraunce.

" Item, thou hast withstoud and maade fences ageynst the Kynges
maiestie, and his lieutenant the worthy Lorde my broder of Warr-
wike; it apperith by the strookes of the greet gunnes in the Kyng

walles of his castell of Bamburghe. For the[se] causes, dispost the to suffre thy penaunce aftyr the lawe. The Kyng had ordenned that thou shuldest have hadd thy sporys striken of by the hard heles, with the hand of the maister cooke, that whiche is here redy to doo, as was promysed at the tyme that he tooke of thy spurres; he said to yee, as ys accustumed, that ' And thou be not true to thy soverain Lord, I shal smyte of thy sporys with this knyf herd by the helys,' and so shewne hym the maistre cooke redy to doo his office, with apron and his knyff.

" Item, Sir Rauff Grey, the Kyng had ordenned here, thou maist see, the Kynge of armes and heroudes, and thine own propre cote of armes, that whiche they shuld teere of thy body, and so thou shuldist as wel be disgraded of thy worshipp, noblesse, and armes, as of the order of Knyghthode; and also here is an oder cote of thin armes reversed, the which thou shuldest have werne of thy body, going to that dethe warde, for that belongethe aftyr the lawe. Notwithstanding, of the disgrading of knygthode, and of thine armes, et noblesse, the King pardons that for thy noble grauntfader, the whiche suffrid trouble for the Kynges moost noble predecesseurs.* Than, Sir Rauf Grey, this shal be thy penaunce,—thou shalt goo on thy feet unto the towneseend, and there thou shalt be laide downe and drawen to a scaffold maade for thee, and that thou shalt have thyne hede smite of thi body, to be buriede in the freres; thi heede where it pleased the Kyng."

P. 4, l. 11—12.—Were takene and afterward behedede. " Quintode-cimo die mensis Maij, apud Exham, decapitati sunt Dux Somersett, Edmundus Fizthu miles, Bradshaw, Wauter Hunt, Blac Jakis. Decimo-septimo die mensis Maii, apud Novum-Castrum, decapitati

---

* Sir Ralph Grey, of Wark, Heton, and Chillingham (lineal ancestor of the Earls of Tankerville, as well as of the present Earl Grey) was the grandson of Sir Thomas Grey, beheaded at Southampton with the Earl of Cambridge, Aug. 5, 1415. See the whole-sheet pedigree of Grey in Raine's North Durham.—J.G.N.

sunt Dominus de Hungarforde, Dominus Roos, Dominus Thomas
Fynderum, Edwardus de la Mare, Nicholaus Massam. Apud Mede-
tham, xviij° die mensis Maii, decapitati sunt Dominus Philippus
Wentworth, Willielmus Penyngton, Warde de Topcliff, Oliverus
Wentworth, Willielmus Spilar, Thomas Hunt, *le foteman Regis Hen-*
rici. Apud Eboracum, xxv° die mensis Maii, decapitati sunt Do-
minus Thomas Husye, Thomas Gosse, Robertus Merfynn, Johannes
Butlerus, Rogerus Water, *janitor Regis Henrici,* Thomas Fenwyke,
Robertus Cocfeld, Willielmus Bryte, Willielmus Dawsonn, Johannes Chapman. Apud Eboracum, xxviij° die mensis Maii, decapitati
sunt Johannes Elderbek, Ricardus Cawerum, Johannes Roselle,
Robertus Conqueror."—*MS. Arundel, Coll. Arm.* 5, fol. 170, r°.

P. 4, *l.* 26.—*Chaunged the coyn of Englonde.* This whole passage is
transcribed by Stowe, nearly word for word, in his Chronicle,
pp. 418—19. " Mense Octobris, fecit Rex proclamare Radingiæ,
et per totam Angliam, quod unum nobile Regis Henrici valeret
viij. s. iiij. d., fecitque novum Cunagium turri Londoniæ, ad summum
dampnum magnatum regni."—*W. Wyrcestre Annales,* p. 500. Cf.
Archæologia, XV. 165; and Sir Henry Ellis's edition of *Grafton's Con-*
tinuation of Harding's Chronicle, p. 437.

—— *l.* 3.—*And also he made angelle noblys of vj. s. viij. d.* i. e. he
made the noble of that price, and changed its name to that of angel;
Hearne's Fragment, p. 294. A very short time previously the noble
was of comparatively trifling value.—*MS. Ch. Ant. Eg.* 88.

P. 5, *l.* 2.—*A blacke monke of Abyngtone.* In the curious fragment
printed by Hearne, at the end of the Chronicle of Sprottus, we are
informed that William Cantlow was the name of this rascal. Henry's
capture, in the MS. N° 5, in the College of Arms, is placed under
the year 1465 :—" Hoc et anno, circiter festum Apostolorum Petri et
Pauli, captus est Henricus Sextus, nuper Rex Anglie, du[c]tus et
publice per Chepam Londonie, cum aliis secum captis; ductus usque
ad Turrim Londonie, ibique honorifice commendatus custodie mansit."
Fol. 170, v°.

P. 5, *l.* 3.—*Bungerley Hyppyngstones.* This was a ford, obtained by stepping-stones, across the river Ribble.—J. G. N.

—— *l.* 4.—*Thomas Talbott, sonne and heyre to Sere Edmund Talbot of Basshalle.* Sir Edmund Talbot, of Bashall, in the parish of Mitton, co. York, died in the 1st Edw. IV. His son, Sir Thomas, was then under age (pedigree in Whitaker's History of Craven, 2d edit. 1812, p. 25); but there can be little doubt that, before his traitorous achievement, he had married Alice, daughter of Sir John Tempest, of Bracewell, under whose protection the unfortunate King was then living. Beside the present reward mentioned in the ensuing note, Sir Thomas Talbot appears to have received a grant of a yearly pension of 40*l.*, which was confirmed by Richard III. (pedigree, as above). He survived to the 13th Hen. VII. His father-in-law, Sir John Tempest, was Sheriff of Yorkshire in 18 and 37 Henry VI. (see pedigree of Tempest in Whitaker's Craven, p. 80.)—J. G. N.

—— *l.* 4.—*Thomas Talbott.* In the Issue Rolls of the Exchequer of 5 Edw. IV. are the statements of monies paid to this gentleman and others for taking Henry, late *de facto et non de jure* King of England. It appears that Sir James Haryngton and Sir John Tempest were also concerned in the capture; but the fact of Sir Thomas Talbot being the chief actor is confirmed by the amount of their relative rewards, he receiving 100*l.* and they each 100 marks. Their " costs and charges," amounting to 100 marks, were also paid. John Levesey also received a reward of 20*l.*, and William Rogers of Serne and David Colinley, valets of the King's chamber, together 6*l.* 13*s.* 4*d.* On the 9th of July 1465, Edward, in consideration of " magnam et laboriosam diligentiam suam circa captionem et retinentiam magni proditoris, rebellis, et inimici nostri Henrici nuper vocati Regis Henrici Sexti, per ipsum Jacobum factum," gave to Sir James Haryngton a grant of Thurland Castle and other lands, formerly belonging to Richard Tunstell,* a partizan of Henry.—*Fœdera*, XI. 548.

* The great extent of these possessions may be seen in the Great Roll of the Pipe for 1 Edw. IV. com. Westmorland.

" My ancestor, Sir James Haryngton, did once take prisoner, with his party, this poor prince ; for which the House of York did graunt him a parcel of lands in the northern counties, and which he was fool enough to lose again, after the battle of Bosworth, when King Henry the Seventh came to the crown."—*Haryngton's Nugæ Antiquæ, by T. Park*, vol. II. pp. 385–86. Cf. *Rot. Parl.* V. 584, and *Devon's Issue Rolls of the Exchequer*, p. 489.

[Sir James Harrington was of Brierley near Barnsley ; a younger brother of Sir John Harrington, of Hornby, who had fallen on the Yorkists' side at the battle of Wakefield in 1460 ; their father, Sir Thomas, dying also of his wounds the day after the same battle. Sir James had, in 6 Edw. IV. a grant of 340*l.* from the issues of the county of York. Both he and his younger brother, Sir Robert Harrington, were attainted after the battle of Bosworth in 1 Hen. VII. See further respecting him in Hunter's Deanery of Doncaster, vol. ii. p. 403 ; to which it may be added that it is probably of him that Leland speaks : " There was a younger brother of the Haryngtons that had in gifte Horneby Castelle." (Itin. viii. f. 109 a.), that is, he had it for a time to the prejudice of his nieces, the heirs of his elder brother.—J. G. N.]

P. 5, *l.* 5.—*Jhon Talbott his cosyne of Colebry.* That is, of Salesbury, in the parish of Blackburn, co. Lancaster ; see Whitaker's Whalley, 3d edit. 1818, p. 432. A yearly fee of twenty marks was granted by King Edward in consideration of the good and faithful service of Johannes Talbot de Salebury, Esq. " in captura magni adversarii sui Henrici," until he received a grant of lands or tenements to the like value ; and the same annuity was confirmed to his son Sir John Talbot, of Salebury, by King Richard the Third. See the grant of the confirmation, dated at York 6th June 1484, printed in Baines's History of Lancashire, vol. i. p. 421.—J. G. N.

—— *l.* 6.—*Whiche disseyvide*, i. e. which King Henry, deceived.

—— *l.* 6.—*Wadyngtone Hall.* Waddington is a chapelry within the parish of Mitton, little more than a mile from Bashall. It had belonged to the Tempests of Bracewell from the time of Edward I. Dr. Whitaker says (Hist. of Craven, p. 25), " Waddington Hall, though constructed of strong old masonry, has nearly lost all appearance of antiquity. But one room contains the name of King Henry's chamber." In the History of Whalley, p. 473, will be seen an etching of the ruins. At Bracewell also, (which is now likewise in ruins,) in the older stone portion of the house, " is an apartment called King Henry's Parlour; undoubtedly one of the retreats of Henry VI." (Ibid. p. 82.) At Bolton, in the same neighbourhood, after describing a very ancient hall, and its canopy over the high table, Dr. Whitaker adds, " In this very hall, and probably under the same canopy, that unhappy monarch ate the bread of affliction during a retreat, as it is reported by tradition, of several months. An adjoining well retains the name of King Harry, who is said to have directed it to be dug and walled, in its present shape, for a cold bath." It is at Bolton where there are still preserved three relics of King Henry, a boot, a glove, and a spoon; figures of which are engraved in the Gentleman's Magazine for June 1785, and again in the History of Craven, p. 106. The boot and glove are remarkably small, and show, in Dr. Whitaker's words, that " in an age when the habits of the great, in peace as well as war, required perpetual exertions of bodily strength, this unhappy prince must have been equally contemptible from corporeal and from mental imbecility."—J. G. N.

P. 5, l. 7, 8.—His lege bownde to the styrope. One author, and as far as I have been able to find he is the only authority for it, says, that Henry was immediately cast into chains.—*Matthæi Palmesii Pisani Continuatio Chronici Eusebiani*, ed. Venetiis, 1483, fol. 155, vo. According to some writers, Henry's two religious friends, Drs. Manning and Bedle, were the only companions of his misfortunes.—Cf. *Monstrelet, IV.* 182.

——, *l. 9.—By the Lorde Harberde.* " Et castrum forte in Wallia per dominum Harbarde captum est, et Dominus Ricardus Tunstalle, cum ceteris ibi inventis, captus est, et in Turri Londonie clausus, qui tum in breve gratiam a Rege consecutus est. Duo nobiles ex illic capti decollati sunt."—*MS. Arundel, Coll. Arm. 5*, fol. 171, ro. There is a grant to Lord Herbert for his services in *Rot. Pat. 3 Edw. IV.*

P. 5, *l.* 16.—*By lawe padowe.* I do not understand the meaning of the word·" Padowe," except it be Paduan.

—— *l.* 22.—*And in vij. yere.* An anonymous scribbler says, that in this year there was, throughout England, a hurricane (*vehementissimus ventus*) which lasted for more than thirty-six hours.—*MS. Arundel, Mus. Brit.* 220. fol. 279, vº.

P. 6, *l.* 4.—*Were takene for treasoune and behedede.* See a valuable and curious note by Mr. Stapleton, in his volume of the Plumpton Correspondence, pp. 18, 19. This happened " circiter octavum Epiphanie."—*MS. Arundel, Coll. Arm.* 5, fol. 171, rº.

—— *l.* 19.—*xliij M¹.* So in MS., but probably a clerical error for xiiij. M¹.

—— *l.* 25.—*A playne byyonde Banbury toune.* Danesmoor is in the parish of Edgecote, near three hills of unequal size, and in their relative position approaching a triangle; " the spot now called Danesmoor is a small plantation of a few acres, but the name at this period had doubtless a much more extended application."—*Baker's Northamptonshire,* I. 500. This battle is commemorated in " Marwnad Thomas ab Rhosser, arglwydd Herast " of Lewis Glyn Cothi. Three things ought to be remarked, viz. that Herbert, who was beheaded, only made a codicil to his will, and not a new one, as commonly stated; that the battle took place on the Monday—

" Dyw Llun y bu waed a lladd :"

and that Herbert and his fellow captives were executed on the Wednesday—

" Marchog a las ddyw Merclur,"

as Gutto Glyn remarks in his poetical language. Cf. MS. Cotton. Otho, B. xiv. fol. 221, vº, where an erroneous date is given to the battle,—*in quo cæsi multa milia.* In MS. Tann. Bodl. 2, fol. 104, vº. we find the field called " prelium ad Hegecote, seu Danysmore, prope Banburiam, dictam *Banbery-Feld,* seu *Hegecote-Fyld.*" Hearne's fragment informs us that the land on which the battle was fought belonged to a person named Clarell. In the valuable collection of manuscripts at the seat of W. Ormsby Gore, Esq. are some verses in the Welsh language on this battle; see Sir Thomas Phillipps's Catalogue of these Manuscripts, p. 1.

P. 6. l. 28, 29.—The names of the gentylmen that were slayne. See another and more extensive list in *Itinerarium Willelmi de Worcestre,* p. 120-1, although the major part of this catalogue differs from his. Worcester says that at least 168 of the nobility and gentry of Wales fell in this battle, and 1500 men on the English side.

—— *l. 30, 31.—Herry Organ, sonne and heyre,* i. e. the son and heir of Henry Organ.

P. 7, l. 5.—Sere Herry Latymere. Rather Sir Henry Neville, paternally a cousin-german of the great Earl of Warwick, and whose mother was Lady Elizabeth Beauchamp, half-sister to the heiress Anne, whom the Earl of Warwick married. Leland, in describing the Beauchamp Chapel at Warwick, says : " There lyeth buried (as some saye) in the west end of our Lady Chapell one of the Nevilles L. Latemer, slayne at Edgcote field by Banbury (as some suppose), but there is neither tombe nor scripture seene. This was Sir Hen. Neville, sonne and heire of George Neville, Lord Latemer. But he was never Lord, for he dyed before his father. This Henry Neville was grandfather to the Lord Latemer now livinge." The fact of Sir Henry Neville, and of his brother-in-law John Dudley, also slain in the same battle, having been buried in the Beauchamp Chapel, is proved by the will of his mother Lady Latimer, who on the field of Edgcote lost her only son and the husband of her daughter. Before the close of the same year, (on the 30th Dec.) her husband died insane. Nichols's Beauchamp Monuments, 4to. p. 40.—J. G. N.

—— *l. 7.—Sir John Conyers of Hornby, com. Ebor. Kt.*

—— *l. 8 —Olivere Audley, squyere.* For Audley read Dudley. He was a son of John Lord Dudley, K.G. and brother of that John who was grandfather of John Duke of Northumberland. Beauchamp Monuments, p. 39.—J. G. N.

—— *l. 11-12.—*" Hic W. Harberde, gravissimus et oppressor et spoliator ecclesiasticorum et aliorum multorum per annos multos, hunc tandem, justo Dei judicio pro suis sceleribus et nequiciis, recepit mercedem. Die Sabbati proximo ante assumpcionem beatissime semper Virginis Marie, captus est Dominus de Rywaus, cum domino Johanne filio suo, et, juxta castrum de Kelingworthe, pariter decollati sunt."—MS. Arundel, Coll. Arm. fol. 171 r°.

P. 7, l. 19.—*A vilage bysyde Northampton.* Stowe calls this village Ulney ; that is, Olney, a market-town in Buckinghamshire, but within twelve miles of Northampton.—J. G. N.

—— l. 31.—*A generalle pardone.* On the 27th of October, Henry Percy of Northumberlond, who had been confined in the Tower, under Lord Dudley, Constable, took the oaths of allegiance and was released.—*Fœdera*, XI. 649.

P. 8, l. 4.—I here insert a very curious and valuable document from a MS. Roll in the Ashmolean Museum at Oxford, N°. 1160, m. 2, d°, et 1, d°.

" *The duc of Clarance, th'archebisshoppe of Yorke, and th'erle of Warwyk.*

" Right trusty and welbelovid, we grete you welle. And welle ye witte that the Kyng oure soveregne lordys true subgettes of diverse partyes of this his realme of Engelond have delivered to us certeyn billis of Articles, whiche we suppose that ye have in thoos parties, rememberynge in the same the disceyvabille covetous rule and gydynge of certeyne ceducious persones ; that is to say, the Lord Ryvers, the Duchesse of Bedford his wyf, Ser William Herbert, Erle of Penbroke, Humfrey Stafford, Erle of Devenshire, the Lordis Scalis and Audeley, Ser John Wydevile, and his brethern, Ser John Fogge, and other of theyre myschevous rule opinion and assent, wheche have caused oure seid sovereyn Lord and his seid realme to falle in grete poverte of myserie, disturbynge the mynystracion of the lawes, only entendyng to thaire owen promocion and enrichyng. The seid trewe subgettis with pitevous lamentacion callyng uppon us and other lordes to be meanes to oure seid sovereyne Lord for a remedy and reformacion ; werfore we, thenkyng the peticioun comprised in the seid articles resonabyll and profitable for the honoure and profite of oure seid sovereyn Lord and the comune welle of alle this his realme, fully purposed with other lordis to shewe the same to his good grace, desiryng and pray you to dispose and arredie you to accompayneye us thedir, with as many persones defensabyly arrayede as y can make, lettyng you wete that by Goddis grace we entende to be at Caunterbury uppon Sonday next comyng. Wretyn undre oure signettis and signe manuell the xijth day of Juyll, A° 1469.

" In three the next articles undrewretin are comprisid and specified the occasions and verry causes of the grete inconveniencis and mischeves that fall in this lond in the dayes of Kyng Edward the ij^{de}, Kyng Ric' the ij^{de}, and Kyng Henry the vj^{te}, to the distruccion of them, And to the gret hurt and empoverysshyng of this lond.

" First, where the seid Kynges estraingid the gret lordis of thayre blood from thaire secrete Councelle, And not avised by them; And takyng abowte them other not of thaire blood, and enclynyng only to theire counselle, rule and advise, the wheche persones take not respect ne consideracion to the wele of the seid princes, ne to the comonwele of this lond, but only to theire singuler lucour and enrichyng of themself and theire bloode, as welle in theire greet possessions as in goodis; by the wheche the seid princes were so enpoverysshed that they hadde not sufficient of lyvelode ne of goodis, wherby they myght kepe and mayntene theire honorable estate and ordinarie charges withynne this realme.

" Also the seid seducious persones, not willing to leve the possessions that they hadde, caused the seid princes to lay suche imposicions and charges as welle by way of untrue appecementes to whom they owed evill wille unto, as by dymes, taxis and prestis noblis and other inordinat charges uppon theire subjettes and commons, to the grete grugge and enpoveryssyng of them, wheche caused alle the people of this lond to grugge.

" And also the seid seducious persones by theyre mayntenaunces, where they have rule, wold not suffre the lawes to be executed, but where they owe favour moved the seid princes to the same; by the wheche there were no lawes atte that tyme deuly ministred, ne putt in execucion, wheche caused gret murdres, roberyes, rapes, oppressions, and extorcions, as well by themself, as by theyre gret mayntenaunces of them to be doon, to the gret grugge of all this lande.

" Hit is so that where the kyng oure sovereigne lorde hathe hadde as gret lyvelode and possessions as evyr had kyng of Engelond ; that is to say, the lyvelode of the Crowne, Principalite of Wales, Duche of Lancastre, Duche of Cornwelle, Duche of York, the Erldome of Chestre, the Erldome of Marche, the Lordeschippe of Irlond, and other, with grete forfaytis, besyde Tunage and Poundage of alle this londe, grauntyd only to the kepynge of the see. The lorde Revers, the Duchesse of Bedford his wyf, and thayre sonnes, Ser William Harbert, Earle of Pembroke, and Humfrey Stafford, Erle of Devonshire, the Lord of Audely, and Ser John Fogge, and other of thayre myschevous assent and oppinion, whiche have advised and causid oure seid sovereigne lord to geve of the seyd lyvelode and possessions to them above theire disertis and degrees, So that he may nat lyf honorably and mayntene his estate and charges ordinarie withinne this lond.

" And also the seid seducious persones next before expressid, not willyng to leve suche large possessions and goodis as they have of oure seid sovereigne lordis gyfte, have, by subtile and discevable ymaginacions, movid and causid oure sovereyne lord to chaunge his most ryche coyne, and mynysshed his most royalle household, to the gret appeycyng of his estate, and the comonwele of this londe.

" Also seid seducious persones, continuyng in theire most deseyvable and covetous disposiscion, have causid oure seid soverayne lord to aske and charge us his trewe comons and subgettis wyth suche gret imposicions and inordinat charges, as by meanes of borowyng withoute payment, takyng goodes of executours of rich men, taxis, dymes, and preestis noblis; takyng gret goodis for his household without payment, impechementes of treasounes to whom they owe any eville will; So that ther can be no man of worshippe or richesse, other spirituelle or temporelle, knyghtis, squiers, marchauntes, or any other honest persone, in surete of his lyf, lyvelode, or goodis; where the seid seducious persones, or any of them, owe any malice or eville wille, to the grete drede and importabylle charges, and the utter empoverysshyng of us his treue Commons and subjettes, And to the gret enrychyng of themself, the premisses amountynge to ccM^l. markes [this yere] and more.

" Also the seid seducious persones have caused our seid sovereygné lord to spende the goodis of oure holy fadir [the pope], the wheche were yevyn hym for defence of Cristen feyth of many goodely disposyd people of this lond, without repayment of oure seid holy fadir, for the wheche cause this lond stondith in juberdie of Enterdytynge.

" Also the seid seducious persones, be thayre mayntenaunces in the cuntreyes where they dwelt or where they here rule, will not suffre the Kynges lawes to be executyd uppon whom they owyd favere unto, And also movid oure seid sovereyne lord to the same ; by the wheche the lawes be not duly mynystered, ne put in execucion ; by the wheche gret murdre, robbres, rapes, oppressions, and extorcions, as well be them, as by thayre gret mayntenaunces of theire servauntes, to us daly done and remayne unpunysshed, to the gret hurt and grugge of alle this londe.

" Also the seid seducious persones hath causid oure seid soverayne lord to estrainge the true lordis of his blood from his secrete Councelle, to th'entent that they myghte atteyne and brenge abought theyre fals and dysceyvable purpos in premisses aforseid, to the gret enrychynge of themself, And to the gret hurt and poverte of oure seid sovereyne lorde, and to alle us his trewe subjettis and commons of this londe."

*" These undrewretyn are the peticions of us treue and feythefulle subjettes
and commons of this lond for the gret wele and surete of the Kyng oure
sovereigne lord and his heires, and the commonwele of this lond, evir to be
contynued. Aftir humble praying of trewe lordis, spirituelle and temporelle, to yeve assistence and aid in thys oure true and goodely desyres ;
For we take God to record we entende but only for the wele and surete of the
Kyng oure sovereigne lord, And the common-wele of this lond.*

" First, that the seid seducious persones abovenamed, wheche by
theire subtile and malicious meanes have causyd oure said sovereyn
lord to estrainge his goode grace from the Councelle of the nobile and
trewe lordis of his blood, moved hym to breke hys lawes and statutis,
mynysshed his lyvelode and housold, chaunchyng his most richest
coyne, and chargyng this lond with suche gret and inordinat imposicions, as is above expressid ; to the grete appeirement of his most
Royalle estate, and enpoverisshyng of hym and alle his true Commons and subjettis, and only to the enrichynge of themself; may be
punysshed accordyng to theire werkes and untrouethes, So that alle
other hereaftir shall take ensample by thayme.

" Also in eschewyng the occasions and causes of the gret inconveniencis and myschevis that by the same hathe fallen in the Kynges
dayes, above expressid, as well uppon themself, as uppon this lond,
And that in tymes hereaftir myghte falle ; We, the Kyngis
true and feithfulle Commons and subjettes of this lond, mekely
besechen his good grace that hit well lyke hym for the gret wele of
hymself, his heires, and the common-wele of us his true subjettes
and Commons, for evyr to be continued by the advyse and auctorite
of his lordis spirituelle and temporalle, to appoynte, ordeyne, and
stablish for evyr to be hadde suche a sufficiente of lyvelode and pos-
sescions, by the whiche he and alle his heires aftir hym may mayntene and kepe theire most honorable estate, withe alle other ordinarie charges necessarye to be hadde in this lond. So that he nor
noon of his heires, hereafter, of necessite, nede to charge and ley
uppon his true Commons and subjettes suche gret imposicions as
before is expressid ; Unlesse that it were for the gret and urgent

causes concernynge as well the wellthe of us, as of oure seid sovereyne lord; Accordyng to the promyse that he made in his last parliament, openly wyth his owen mouthe unto us.

" Also to be enstablisshid be the seid auctorite, that yf any persone, of what estate or degree that he be, aftir the seid stablisshement so ordeyned, and made, (except the Kynges issue and his brethern), presume or take uppon them to aske or take possessions of any of the lyvelod so appoyntyd, that, by the seid auctorite, he be taken and reputyd as he that wold mynysshe and apeire the royall estate of his sovereyn lord, and the commonwele of this lond.   And went pardon so to be punysshed.

" Also that the revenues of Tounage and Poundage may be employed in the kepyng of the see as it was grauntod, and too non other use, for the safetie of entrecourse of merchaundizes, to gret enrichyng of this lond, and also for the defence of the enemyes.

" Also that the lawes and the statutis made in the dayes of youre noble progenitours kyng Edward the iij^de., sethen for the concernyng and kepyng of this lond in good hele and peas, as welle Wales as Engelond, be duly kept, observid, and executyd, for the conservacion of us youre trewe commons and subjettes in peas, and the commonwele of this oure lond."

P. 8, l. 5.—And in the x. yere.   It may be remarked that the regnal years of Edward IV. commence on the fourth of March, " quo die Rex Edwardus iiij^tus. incepit regnare;"—MS. Magnus Rotulus Pipæ, 1 Edw. IV, com. Cornub. Cf. MS. Bib. Geo. III. Mus. Brit. 52. fol. 33, r°.

—— *l. 6.—The Lorde Welles his sonne.*   See the *Excerpta Historica,* p. 282, for the confession of Sir Robert Welles, which throws very considerable light on this history.   It appears that the Duke of Clarence took a much more active part in the conspiracy than is generally supposed; that the motive which actuated the multitude was chiefly the fear of the King's vengeance; that a servant of Clarence's was in the battle, and afforded Welles considerable assist-

tance; that when Lord Welles went to London pursuant to the
King's commands, he desired his son, in the event of his hearing that
he was in danger, to hasten to his assistance with as many followers
as possible; that the real object of the rebellion was to place the
crown on Clarence's head; and that both Clarence and Warwick
had, for some time, been urging Lord Welles, and his son, to continue firm to their cause.

The following documents are given from the Close Rolls of 10
Edw. IV. (m. 8. dorso.) and are valuable illustrations of the history
of this insurrection.

" *De proclamationibus faciendis.*—Rex vicecomiti Warr' et Leicestr'
salutem.   Præcipimus tibi firmiter injungentes, quod statim, post
receptionem præsentium, in singulis locis infra ballivam, tuam tam
infra libertates quam extra, ubi magis expediens videris, ex parte
nostra publicas proclamationes fieri facias, in hæc verba—

" For as moche as hit hath plesyd God, of his godeness and grace,
to send to our soveraigne Lord the victorye of his Rebelles and Traitours of his shire of Lincolne, late assembled in grete nombre, leveyng
werre ayenst his Highness, contrary to their ligeaunce and duete;
Oure said Soveraigne Lord, therefore, not willing his subgettis, other
than such as now attend upon his most Royall Person, to be putte
to charge, labour, and businesse, by vertue of his commissions of
array, and other writing, late addressed to dyvers shires, citees, and
townes, for the resistens of the malicious and traiterous purpose of the
said Rebelles, wolle, and in the most straitest wise chargeth, that
noon of his subgettes presume, ne take uppon hym, to ryse, ne make
any assemble or gadering, by reason of any of the seid commissions
or writings, ne be moeving, steryng, writing, or commaundement
made, or hereafter to be made, by any persone or persones of what
estate, degree, or condition sooever he be of, lesse than hit bee by the
Kinges commission, Prive Seal, or writyng under his signet, of new
to be made aftir this the xiij. day of Marche.   And if any persone or
persones presume, or take uppon theym or hym, to doe the contrary

hereof, Our Said Soveraigne Lord woll repute and take hym and them soo doyng as his ennemyes and Rebelles, and wool procede to their lawfull Punycion in the most streitest wise, according to his Lawes and Statutes in such case ordeyned.

" Et hoc nullatenus omittas. Teste Rege apud Stamford xiij°. die Martii.

" PER IPSUM REGEM."

(Here follow the names of counties.)

" *De proclamationibus faciendis.*—Rex vicecomiti Eborum salutem. Præcipimus tibi, quod statim post receptionem presentium, in singulis locis infra ballivam tuam, tam infra libertates quam extra, ubi magis expediens videris, ex parte nostra publicas proclamationes fieri facias in hæc verba—

" Howbeit that the King our Soveraine Lord graunted unto Georg Duc of Clarence, and Richard Erle of Warwyk, his pardon generall of all offences committed and doon ayenst him, afore the fest of Christmasse last passed, trusting thereby to have caused theym to have shewed unto him their naturall love, ligeaunce, and duetie, and to have assisted his Highness, as well in subdueing insurrections and rebellions late made ayenst him in the countie of Lincolne, as in all other things concerning the suertie of his persone ; and, in trust that they soo wold have done according to their promisses to hym made, his said Highness auctorized theym by his commission undre his grete seal to assemble his subgetts in certain shires, and theym to have brought to his said Highnes, to the entent aforesaid ; yet the said Duc and Erle, unnaturally, unkindly, and untruly intending his destruction and the subversion of his reaume, and the common-wele of the same, and to make the said Duke King of this his said Reaume, ayenst Gods law, mannes law, and all reason and conscience, dissimiled with his seid Highness, and, under colour thereof, falsly and traiterously provoked and stured, as well by their writings as otherwise, Sir Robert Welles, late calling himselfe Great Capitayne of the Commons of the seid shire of Lincolne, to continue the said insurrections and rebellions, and to levee warre ayenst hym, as they, by the same, soe dyd with banners displayed, avauncing theymselfe in plain bataylle, unto the time his said Highnesse, by the help of God, put them to flight ; wherein the said Duc and Erle promitted to the said Sir Robert and Commons to have yeven them their assistences to the uttermost of their powers, and soo wolde have done, if God ne had yeven unto hym the said victorie, as the same Sir Robert Welles, Sir Thomas de la Laund, Richard Wareyn, and other have openly confessed and shewed before his seid Highnes, the Lordes of his blood, and the multitude of his subgettis attending upon hym in his host at this tyme ; which Sir Robert Welles, and the said other pety capitaynes, affirmed to be true at their dethes, uncompelled, unstirred, or undesired soo to doo ; and as by the confession of the said Robert Welles, made under his writing and signe manuell, it apperith. And after that the said Duc and Erle, understanding and seing that this ther seid labours wold not serve to the perfourmyng of their fals and traiterous purpose afore declared, laboured by their writings and messages sent into Yorkeshire into divers persons there, theym straitly charging to doo make open proclamations in their owne names, without making mention of his seid Highnes, that all maner men upon peyn of deth shuld come unto theym, and yeve theym their assistences in resisting of hym; whereupon his seid Highnes sent unto the said Duc and Erle, by Garter King of Armes, summonicion and warnyng of their said accusations undir his prive seal, straitly charging theym to come unto his said Highnes, resonably accompanyed according to their astates and degrees, to answer unto their said accusations ; which to doo they presumptuously refused, and withdrew themselfe, and fled with their felaship into Lancashire ; soo as his said Highness with his host for lak of vitaill might not follow them, to the intent that they might gadre his subgettes in gretter nombre, and to be able to performe their said fals and traiterous purpose and entent; for the which causes they have deserved to be published as fals traitours and rebelles, and to have the uttermost punition of the law; yet, nathelesse, our said Soveraigne Lord considering the nighness of blood that they be of unto him, and the tendre love which he hath afore time borne to theym, were therefore loth to lese theym, if they wold submitt theym to his grace, and put hym in suertie of their good demeaning hereafter.

" Wherefore our said Sovereigne Lord woll, and in the most straitest wyse chargeth, the said Duc and Erle, that they, in their persones, come in humble and obeysant wyse, and appier afore his Highnes the xxviij. day of this present month of March, Wednesday next, or afore, wheresoever he than shall be, to answer unto the said accusations; which if they woll soo doo, and come declare theymselfe nat guilty, his Highness woll be thereof right glad, and have hem in his grace and favour; and if they refuse thus to doo, then our said Soveraigne Lord reputeth, taketh, and declareth thaym as his rebelles and traitoures, willing and straitly charging all his subgetts to doo the same, and that noon of his subgetts from that time forth receive theym, ne eyther of theym ayd, favour, or assist with mete, drink, ne money, or otherwise, ne noon other persone which, after the said Duc and Erle have refused to come to our said Soverain Lord as is aforesaid, abydeth with theym, or aydeth theym, or assisteth in any wise ; but that every of the King's subgetts putte hem in effectuell devir to take the said Duc and Erle, and all other soo abyding with theym, or aiding or assisting theym, as is abovesaid, and theym suerly bring to his Highnes uppon peyn of deth ; And he that taketh and bringeth the said Duc or Erle shall have for his reward, to hym and his heires, an C. li. worth of his lond of yerely value, or Ml. li. in redy money, at his election ; and for a knyght xx.li. worth of his lond, or C. marc in money ; and for a squyer x. li. worth of his lond, or xl. li. in money ; and over that cause our said soveraigne Lord to have hym and theym soo doing in the more tendre favour of his good grace at all tymes hereafter.

" Et hoc sub periculo incumbenti nullatenus omittas.   Teste Rege
apud Eborum xxiiij° die Martii.

" PER IPSUM REGEM.

" Consimilia brevia diriguntur vicecomitibus in Com' subscriptis
sub data predicta, videlicet,

" Majori et vicecomitibus Civitatis London'." (&c.)

" Rex Vicecomiti Eborum Salutem.   Præcipimus tibi firmiter injungentes, quod, statim post receptionem præsentium, in singulis locis
infra ballivam tuam, tam infra libertates quam extra, ubi magis expediens videris, ex parte nostra publicas proclamationes fieri facias,
in hæc verba—

" Howbeit that the King our Soveraigne Lord graunted unto
Georg Duke of Clarence, and Richard Earl of Warrewyk, his pardon generall of all offences committed and doone ayenst him, afore
the fest of Cristemasse last past ; trusting thereby to have caused
theym to have shewed unto hym theyr naturall love, ligeaunce, and
duetee, and to have assisted his Highnesse, as well in subdueing insurrections and rebellyons late made ayenst him in the Counte of
Lincolne, as in all other things concerning the suertee of his persone ;
and in trust that they wold soo have done according to their promisses to hym made, his said Highnesse auctorised theym, by his
commission under his great seall, to assemble his subgietts in certain
shires, and them to have brought unto his said Highnesse, to th'entent aforesaid ; yet the said Duke and Erle unnaturally, unkindely, and
untruly entending his destruction, and the subversion of his reaume,
and the commonwele of the same, and to make the seid Duke King
of this his said Reaume, ayenst God's lawe, mannes lawe, all reason
and conscience, dissimiled with his said Highness ; and under colour
thereof, falsly and traiterously provoked, laboured, and stured, as
well by their writings as otherwise, Sir Robert Welles, late calling
himselfe Grete Capitayne of the commons of the said Shire of Lincolne,

to continue the said insurrections and rebellions, and to levee werre
ayenst him, as they by the same soo did, with banners displayed,
avauncing theymselfe in pleyn bataille, unto the time his said
Highness, by the help of God, put theym to flyght; wherein the
said Duke and Erle promytted to the said Sir Robert and Commons
to have yeven theym their assistences to the uttermost of their powers,
and soo wold have doone, yf God ne had yeven unto hym the said
victorye, as the same Sir Robert Welles, Sir Thomas de la Laund,
Richard Waryng, and other, have openly confessed and shewed before his said Highness, the Lordes of his blode, and the multitude of
his subgietts attending upon him in his host at this time ; which Sir
Robert Welles, and the other pety Captaynes, affermed to be true at
their dethes, uncompelled, unstured, or undesired soo to doe ; and as
by the confession of the said Sir Robert Wells, made under his
writyng and sign manuell, it appereth ; and after that the said Duke
and Erle, understanding and seing that this ther said labours wold
not serve in the performing of their fals and traiterous purpose, afore
declared, laboured, by their writings and messages sent into Yorkeshire to dyvers persones there, theym streitly charging to doo make
open proclamations in their owne names, without mention makeing
of his said Highness, that all manner men, uppon peyn of deth,
should come unto theym, and yeve theym their assistence in resisting
of him ; whereupon his said Highnesse sent unto the said Duke
and Erle, by Garter Kyng of Armes, summonition and warnyng of
their said accusations undre his privie seal, straitly charging theym
to come unto his said Highness resonably accompanyed, according
to their astates and degrees, to answere to their said accusations ;
which to doo they presumptuously refused, and withdrewe themselfe,
and fled with their felaship into Lancashire, soo as his said Highness
with his host, for lake of vitayl, might not follow theym, to th'entent
that they might gather his subgetts in greter noumbre, and to be
hable to perfourme their said fals and trayterous purpose and entent ;
ffor which causes they have deserved to be published as fals traitours

and rebells, and to have the uttermost punytion of the lawe. Yet nathelesse our said soveraigne Lord considered the nyghnesse of of blode which they be of unto him, and the tender love which he hath afore time borne to theym, therefore was loth to have lost theym, yf they would have submitted theym to his grace, and to have put hym in suertee of their good beryng hereafter; wherefore he sent his writts of proclamation unto dyvers open places, straitly charging theym to have come and appered in their persones afore his Highness in humble and obeysaunt wyse, the xxviij^th. day of this present month of Marche or before, to have aunswered unto the said accusations, shewing by the same that yf they soo would have done, and could have declared theymselfe not guilty, his Highness would have be therewith right gladd, and have had theym in his grace and favour, and that, though they soo cowde not have doon, yet his Highness would not have forgeten their seid nighness of blode, ne the love and favour that he aforetime bare to theym, but wold have ministred to theym ryghtwyssely his lawes with favour and pitee shewyng; which they did not, but obstinately refused soo to doo, and dayly aftir withdrew theymself more and more from his Highness; and after the said proclamations, made as before, it hath be evidently shewed by open confessions made at his citee of Yorke, afore our said Soveraigne and his Lordes than there being with hym, by dyvers persones of grete reputation, that the seid Duke and Erle intended the finall destruction of his most royall persone, and the subversion of this his reaume, and the commonwele of the same, which confessions the said persones have affirmed by their solempne othes, made upon the receyving of the blessed sacrament, to bee faithfull and true; wherefore, the præmisses considered, and the grete obstinacy which they shewed hemself to be of, and yet doo contrarye to their ligeaunce, faith, and duetee, our said soveraigne Lord, to the example of all other like offenders, reputeth, taketh, and declareth the said Duke and Erle as his Rebelles and Traytours, willing and straitly charging all his subgetts to doo the same; and that noon of

his said subgetts from hensforth receyve theym, ne eyther of theym,
ayd, favour, or assist with mete, drynke, or money, or otherwise ;
nor noo other persone beyng with, or adhering to them, or either of
theym, but that every of his said subgetts putt hem in effectuell de-
voyr to take the said Duke and Erle, and the seid persones soe being
with hem, or adhering to theym, or either of theym, and hem surely
bring to the King, upon peyn of deth, and forfaiture of all that they
may forfait ; and he that soo doth shall have for his reward of either
of theym C. li. worth of land by yere to him, and to his heires, or a
$м^l$. li. in redy money at his election.

" Et hoc nullatenus omittas. Teste meipso apud Notingham xxxj°.
die Martii.

" PER IPSUM REGEM."
(Here follow the names of counties.)

(From Madox's transcripts in the British Museum. MS. Add.
4614.)

P. 8, l. 24.—Wove. So in MS. for *vowe.*

P. 9, l. 32.—Kynge Henry schuld rejoyse the kyngdome. " On halmesse
evyn, abowt thre after noyne, comyn into the Comowne Howus, the
Lordys spiritual and temporal, excepte the Kyng, the Duk of York,
and hys sonys ; And the Chawnceler reherset the debate had bytwyn
owre soveren Lord the Kyng and the Duk of York upon the tytelys
of Inglond, Fraunce, and the Lordschep of Erlond, wyche mater was
debat, arguet, and disputet by the seyd lordes spiritual and temporal
byfore owre soveren Lord and the Duk of York longe and diverse
tymys. And at the last, by gret avyce and deliberacion, and by the
assent of owre soveryn Lord and the Duk of York, and alle the
lordes spiritual and temporal ther assemelyd by vertu of thys present
parlement, assentyt, agreyt, and acordyt, that owre sovereyne Lord
the Kyng schal pessabylly and quyetly rejoys and possesse the
crowne of Inglond and of Fraunce and the Lordchip of Irlond, with
al hys preemynences, prerogatyves, and liberteys duryng hys lyf.
And that after hys desese the coroun, etc. schal remayne to Rychard

Duk of York, as rythe inheryt to hym, and to hys issue, prayng and desyring ther the comownes of Inglond, be vertu of thys present parlement assemylet, to comyne the seyd mater, and to gyff therto her assent. The wyche comyns, after the mater debatet, comynt, grawntyt, and assentyt to the forseyd premisses. And ferthermore was granted and assentyt, that the seyd Duk of York, the Erl of March, and of Rutlond, schul be sworne that they schuld not compas ne conspyrene the kynges deth ne hys hurt duryng hys lyf. Ferthermore the forseyd Duk schulde be had, take, and reportyt as eyr apparent prince and ryth inheryter to the crowne aboveseyd. Ferthermore for to be had and take tresoun to ymagyne or compas the deth or the hurt of the seyd Duk, wythe othyr prerogatyves as long to the prince and eyr parawnt. And fferthermore the seyd Duk and hys sonys schul have of the Kyng yerly x.M¹. marces, that is to sey, to hemself v.M¹., to the Erl of Marche iijM¹., the Erl of Rutlond ijM¹. marces. And alle these mateyrs agreyd, assentyt, and inactyt by the auctorite of thys present parlement. And ferthermore, the statutes mad in the tyme of Kyng Herry the fowrth, wherby the croune was curtaylet to hys issu male, utterly anullyd and evertyth, wyth alle other statutes and grantys mad by the seyd Kynges days, Kyng Herry the V. and Kyng Herry the vj^te, in the infforsyng of the tytel of Kyng Herry the fourth in general."—Rot. Harl. C. 7, Membr. 4, *dorso.*

The following document, from Chart. Antiq. Cotton. XVII. 11, is exceeding curious, and I take the opportunity of inserting it here.

" *Jhesus. Maria. Johannes.*

.... the most nobylle and Crysten prynce, oure most dradde soverayne Lorde Kynge Hary the syxte, verrey true undoutyde Kynge of Englonde and of Fraunce, nowe beynge in the hondys of hys rebellys and gret en[e]my, Edwarde, late the Erl of Marche, usurpur, oppressour, and distroyer of oure seyde Soverayn Lorde, and of the nobylle blode of the reme of Englonde, and of the trewe commenes

of the same, by hys myschevus and inordinate newe founden lawes
and ordenaunces inconveniant, to the uttyrmoste destruccion of the
goode commenes of the seyde reme of Englonde; yf yt so schulde
contenne ffor the reformacion wherof, in especialle for the comen-
welle of alle the seyde reme, the ryȝt hyghe and myȝty Prynce
George Duke [of] Clarens, Jasper Erl of Penbroke, Richarde Erl
of Warewyke, and Johnne Erl of Oxenforde, as verrey and trewe
feyȝtfulle cosyns, subgettes, and liege men to oure seyde soveraine
Lorde Kynge Harry the syxt, by sufficiante autorite commysyd unto
theme in thys behalfe, be the hole voyse and assent of the moste
nobylle pryncesse Margaret, Quene of Englonde, and the Ryȝt Hyȝe
and myȝty Prynce Edwarde, atte thys tyme beyng Quene,* into thys
reme to putte theme in ther moste uttermoste devers to dylyver oure
seyd Sopheraine Lord oute of hys grete captivite, and daungere of
hys enmyes, unto hys liberte, and by the grace of Gode to rest hym
in his rialle estate, and crowne of thys hys seyd reme of Englond,
and reforme . . . . . and amende alle the grete myschevus oppressions,
and alle odyr inordinate abusions, nowe raynynge in the seyde reme,
to the perpetualle pese, prosperyte, to the comene welfare of thys
reme. Also ytt ys fully concludyd and grauntyde that alle mail
men within the reme of Englonde, of whatt estat, degre, condicion
that they be of, be fully pardonede of alle maner tresoun or trespace
imagenyd or done, in eny maner of wyse contrary to ther legeyns,
agayne oure soveraine Lorde the Kynge, the Quene, and my Lorde
the prynce, before the day of comynge and entre of the sayde Duke
and Erles in thys sayde reme; so that they putte ihem in ther uttermost dever, and att thys tyme drawe them to the compeny of the
seyde Duke and Erles, to helpe and to fortefy theme in ther purpose
and jorney; excepte suche persons as be capitalle enmyes to oure
seyde soferaine Lorde, withowte punyschement of the whyche god
pece and prosperite of thys reme cannatte be had; and excepte alle
suche as atte thys tyme make any rescistens ageyns the seyde Duke

* This sentence is transposed in the document.

and Erlys, or eny of theme, or of ther compeny. Also the sayde Duke and Erlys, in the name and behalfe of oure seyde soferaine Lorde Kynge Harry the syxt, chargyne and commawndyne that alle maner of men, that be betwen xvj. yeres and lx^{ti}., incontinently and immediatly aftyr thys proclamacion made, be redy, in ther best aray defensabell, to attende and awayte upponne the sayde Duke and Erlys, to aschyst theme in ther jorney, to the entente afore rehercyd, upponne payne of dethe and forfiture of alle that they [may forfeyte], withinne the reme of Englond ; excepte suche persons as be visette with syknesse, or with suche noune poure that they may not go."

P. 10, *l.* 12.—*Inhabytauntes.* So in MS. for *inheritaunces.*

P. 11, *l.* 12.—The Harl. MS. 7353, is a most curious roll on vellum, containing pictures on one side representing parts of scripture history, and on the other assumed similar transactions in the life of Edward IV. We have, I. The King on his throne. II. The King encouraging his soldiers. III. The King with a triple sun shining upon him through three golden crowns, and saying " Domine ! quid vis me facere ?" IV. Pardoning Henry after the battle of Northampton. V. Setting sail for Calais. At the bottom is a genealogical tree, with portraits of all the members of the houses of York and Lancaster, very fantastically arranged.

—— *l.* 12.—*Duke of Burgeyne.* Charles the Bold, Duke of Burgundy, married Edward's sister on the 18th of June, 1467. It was to this marriage that Edward owed his preservation abroad, and the final recovery of his kingdom. An account of the marriage, with the reception of the Princess in Flanders, may be seen in MS. Cotton. Nero, C. IX. Cf. Cart. Antiq. Mus. Brit. XI. 54.

—— *l.* 22.—*Wrott in alle his lettres.* Cf. MS. Harl. 7, fol. 64, r°; Sir Harris Nicolas's Chronology of History, p. 304; Cart. Antiq. Mus. Brit. XXII. 42.

P. 12, *l.* 5.—*Was lost in his tyme.* This was a never-failing source of rebuke against Henry ; so Ocland says—

> " Quippe erat Henricus quintus, dux strenuus olim,
> Mortuus   hinc damni gravior causa atque doloris."

Anglorum prælia. Edit. 1582. Edward, in one of his earlier proclamations, says, " HE that directeth the hertes of all Princes" hath
" putte in oure remembraunce the lamentable state and rayne of this
reaume of Englond, and the losse of th'obeissaunce of the reaume of
Fraunce, and Duchies of Guyenne, and Normandie, and Anjou."
Rot. Claus. 1 Edw. IV. m. 38, dorso.

P. 12, *l.* 26.—*Revertimini,* &c. This is perhaps quoted from memory,
for the reading in the Latin Vulgate is *Convertimini filii revertentes,*
dicit Dominus, quia ego vir vester; which is thus translated,—"Turn,
O backsliding children, saith the Lord, for I am married unto you ;".
Jeremiah, iii. 14. It is almost unnecessary to remark that this is
the sermon with which it was usual to preface the opening of a parliament; the present one was most admirably fitted for the occasion.

P. 13, *l.* 6.—*Was behedede.* " His diebus captus est ille trux carni-
fex, et hominum decollator horridus, Comes de Wacester, et in
Turri Londonie incarceratus, et in breve prope dictam turrim decapi-
tatus, et apud Fratres Predicatores, juxta Ludgate, obscure sepultus."
—MS. Arundel, Coll. Arm. 5, fol. 171, v°. This coming from a
partizan of the same side with the Earl, at a period when party
politics necessarily ran so high, is strikingly conclusive of that nobleman's character. Cf. Chron. p. 9, l. 13—21.

—— *l.* 30.—*At Ravenyspore.* See Mr. Jones's Essay on the Rival
Roses, p. xxv.

P. 14, *l.* 11.—*Nevere wulde clayme no titlc.* He took a solemn oath
to that effect; Cf. MS. Sloan. 3479, and MS. Harl. 2408.

—— *l.* 21.—Ml. Ml. i. e. two thousand.

P. 15, *l.* 18.—*And in dyner tyme Kynge Edwarde was late in.* Edward
was admitted into London on the 11th of April. The Archbishop
suffered himself to be taken at the same time, but was released in two
days afterwards, and obtained full pardon. There is one remarkable
circumstance in this pardon; it remits all crimes before April the
13th, and yet is dated April the 10th, the day probably on which the
Archbishop agreed with Edward to admit him into the city. See

Carte's History of England, book 13, p. 787, *n.*, and *Fœdera,* XI. 709. Warkworth remarks very strongly upon his conduct at p. 26 of his Chronicle. Cf. MS. Bib. Coll. Trin. Oxon. 62 (10).

P. 16, *l.* 14.—*The sunne with stremys.* The crest of the Kynaston coat is supposed to have been assumed from this time, and in allusion to this event.

——— *l.* 29, 30.—*And ther was slayne.* A very comprehensive list is given in MS. Arundel, Mus. Brit. 28, fol. 25, v°. The brass matrix of the seal of the Earl of Warwick, taken from him when he was slain, is in the British Museum ; an impression may be seen among the charters, xxxiv. 33.

P. 17, *l.* 6.—*Lord Barnes sonne and heyre.* Sir Humphrey Bourchier. His gravestone remains in Westminster Abbey, denuded of his figure in brass plate, but retaining an epitaph of fourteen Latin hexameters, commemorative of his prowess and the scene of his death. They commence—

> Hic pugil ecce jacens, Bernett fera bella cupiscens,
> Certat ut Eacides, &c. &c.

See engravings in Gough's Sepulchral Monuments, vol. II. pl. LXXXVI ; Harding's Antiquities in Westminster Abbey, pl. VIII. It may be remarked that the word in the eighth line read *parvulus* by Gough, &c. is really *p*ι*mulus,* i. e. *primulus,* used instead of *primus* for the sake of the metre.—J. G. N.

——— *l.* 7.—*Lord Say.* This nobleman was formerly on the Lancastrian side, but received Edward's pardon on the 5th of May, 1462 ; Chart. Antiq. Mus. Brit. VIII. 13.

——— *l.* 31-2.—*Kynge Herry was put into the Toure ayene.* See *Devon's Issue Rolls of the Exchequer,* p. 491.

P. 18, *l* 1.—*And gaderet grete peple.* Bouchet, in *Les Annales d'Acquitaine,* says that there were *plus de lx. mil hommes armez.* Edit. Par. 1558, fol. 121, v°.

——— *l.* 8.—*And ther he made a felde.* The place where the battle of Tewkesbury was fought is now called Glaston Meadow.—*Rudder's History of Gloucestershire,* p. 736. I have been further assured that this field is now called the *Bloody-Field* by the common people living near the spot.

. P. 18, *l.* 16.—Cf. *Memoires Olivier de la Marche. Edit. Brux.* 1616, p. 502.

—— *l.* 19.—*And there was slayne in the felde Prynce Edward.*— " Confectus apud Tewkysbery per Edwardum Regem quartum." Rot. Harl. C. 7, Memb. 5.

P. 19, *l.* 3, 4.—*Were behedede.* The prior of St. John's in Smith-field was among them.—MS. Arund. Coll. Arm. 5, fol. 171, v°.

—— *l.* 4.—*Noʒtwithstondynge the Kynges pardon.* Edward's policy was despotic in the extreme ; he told De Comines that it was his object to spare the common people, but cut off the gentry. The de-struction of these noblemen and gentlemen was an awful example of his barbarity, as well as his deficiency of common honesty.

—— *l.* 28.—*At Algate and at London Brygge.* " Super pontem Londonie, cum dominibus quibusdam adjacentibus, combusserunt, et similiter alias juxta Algate succederunt."—MS. Arundel, Coll. Arm. 5, fol. 171, v°. In MS. Arundel, Mus. 28, fol. 25, v°, this event is stated to have taken place on the 14th of May, — xiiij°. die mensis Maij supra dict' ; the anonymous scribbler of the notes in this MS. informs us that Lord Rivers put the Bastard to flight.

P. 20, *l.* 9.—*Juperdy,* i. e. jeopardy.

—— *l.* 15.—See this proverb illustrated in Sir Walter Scott's novel of the Abbot, iii. 91-2.

—— *l.* 19.—*Was behedede.* This event took place two days before Michaelmas day in the same year, and his head was placed upon London Bridge "lokyng into Kent warde."—*Paston Correspondence,* ii. 82. Cf. MS. Arundel, Mus. Brit. fol. 25, v°.

P. 21, *l.* 1, 2.—*And ther he was worschipfully receyvid.* " Eodem mensis Maii die xxj°. rediit Rex Edwardus ad civitatem Londonie, cum nobili triumpho."—MS. Arundel, Mus. Brit. 28, fol. 25, v°. The same writer says that he brought Queen Margaret with him *in curru precedente exercitum.* In this triumph he was accompanied by the

Dukes of Clarence, Gloucester, Norfolk, Suffolk, and Buckingham; also the Earls of Northumberland, Shrewsbury, Rivers, Essex, Worcester, Pembroke, &c. See the long list given in the same MS.

P. 21, *l.* 4.—*Was putt to dethe.* " He dyid put to silence in the Tour of London, the xxj. day of May, a°. 1471, buryid first at Chertesey and after at Wyndesore."—Rot. Lansd. Mus. Brit. 6. In the old ballad of the " Wandering Jew's Chronicle" this event is thus versified :—

> " I saw the white and red rose fight,
> And Warwick gret in armour bright,
>   In the Sixth Henries reign ;
> And present was that very hour,
> When Henry was in London Tower,
>   By Crookt-backt Richard slain."

But this subject has been so much before the reader that I refrain from adding more. I give, however, a few references, from my miscellaneous notes, which may assist any future inquirer who desires to investigate more at length into various matters connected with the popular opinion of Henry VI. after his death, his burial places, &c. :—*Widmore's History of Westminster Abbey*, pp. 118-120; *Ashmole's History of the Order of the Garter*, p. 136; MS. Cotton. Cleop. E. 111; *Monast.* I. 277; *British Topographer*, II. 112, n; *Gent. Mag.* LVI.; MS. Cole Collect. XLII. 378; ib. XIII; *Hormanni Vulgaria, Lond.* 1519, fol. 3, r°; *Barrington on the Statutes,* p. 253; *Parker Antiq. Brit. Eccl.* 229, edit. Drake, p. 447; *Fuller's Church History,* IV. 153; *Wilkins's Concil.* IV. 635; *Spelman*, II. 720; *Walpole's Fugitive Pieces;* MS. Sloan. 1441.

—— *l.* 11.—*Caryed to Chyrchesey Abbey in a bote.* Henry's body was protected by soldiers from Calais, and, rather singularly, for the possession of that city had been a hard point of contention between the rival parties. The extreme anxiety of Queen Margaret to possess it, may be seen from a very curious document now preserved in the Royal Archives of France, and the title of which is given in MS. Addit. Mus. Brit. 9346, fol. 116, r°.

In the Issue Rolls of the Exchequer, we find money paid to Hugh Brice on the 24th of June for the expenses of Henry's funeral, for conveying his body from the Tower to St. Paul's, and from thence to Chertsey. From these and several other statements of expences in the same rolls, it fully appears that every respect was paid to the corpse; but Mr. Devon has attempted to draw from this an argument for the natural death of the King, not taking into consideration that the very fact of much attention having been paid to his funeral obsequies would render it more than probable that it was done to conceal the appearance of any hostile feeling: had Henry died a natural death, it appears to me that the haste of Edward's departure into Kent, and the length of time necessarily elapsing before he could have become acquainted with the news, would have almost rendered any definite orders for his funeral next to impossible. Many writers have committed the error of affirming that Henry was buried without honours.—*Camden's Britannia, edit. Gough,* I. 167.

P. 21, *l.* 14.—The names of these aldermen are given by Stowe, Edit. 1755, *Survey of London,* II. 222.

—— *l.* 23.—*One Fauntt of Canterbury.* In the Issue Roll of the Exchequer, 11 Ed. IV. we find the sum of 1*l.* 3*s.* 4*d.* paid to one John Belle, for the value of a horse and harness to conduct this Nicholas Faunte from the Tower of London to the King, then in Kent. Hasted is one of the very few writers who quotes Warkworth's Chronicle, which he does on this point.—*History of Kent,* IV. 433.

In the Introduction I have extracted from Lidgate's poem on the Kings of England; and, for want of a better situation, I here give another version of the stanzas on the reigns of Henry VI. and Edward IV. from a MS. of the commencement of the sixteenth century:—

" The vj[th] Henry his sone was after him fosterde in all vertu,
By just titull and by inheritaunce,
By grace afore provyde of Criste Jhesu,
To were ij crownes bothe in Inglande and in Fraunce.

Above erthly thingis all God was in his remembraunce ;
What vertuus lyfe he led his myraculis now declare !
xxxix. yere he bare dyadym and septure,
In Wyndesore College of the Garter he lyethe in his sepulture.

" After Henry the vjth, Goddis campyoun and trewe knyght,
   Edward the iiijth obteynede Septure and Crowne,
   From the by Plantagenate havynge titule and right,
   xxij. yere the saide Edwarde flowerede withe wysdome, riches and renowne.
   Grete welthe and plente in his dayes all penery put downe,
   All Cristyn princes were glade withe hym amyte to make,
   Whiche onely with a loke made Fraunce and Scotlande to quake ;
   In the College of the Garter where he governoure was and hede,
   He chase the place of his sepulture, for his body to be beriede in when he was dede."

                        MS. Bib. Reg. 18 D. II. fol. 182. v°.

This version is completely remodelled ; the MS. Sloan. 1986 (fol. 199, r°.—213, v°.) contains another different edition of the fifteenth century.

P. 22, *l.* 7.—*The most mervelous blasynge sterre.* See an account of this comet in the Nuremburgh Chronicle, Edit. 1493, fol. 254, r°. " Longum radium in modum flamme ingentis ignis emittens."—MS. Arundel, Mus. Brit. 220, fol. 279, v°. This comet is a return of the one described in a manuscript of the fourteenth century in Sion College Library (xix. 2, fol. 155, v°, b.), and of which there is a drawing on fol. 155, v°, a. Cf. MS. Trin. Cantab. R. xv. 18; Bib. Publ. Cantab. KK. IV. 7.; MS. Cotton. Jul. F. xi.

I give the following fragment relative to this comet from a MS. in the library of Pembroke College, Cambridge :—

        " *De opinionibus aliquorum de presenti cometa.*

" Quidam presumpcionis filius in consulto sermone procacique oracione, volgari verbo tenus ornata, preter phisicas et astrologicas tradiciones, quas tamen similabat, terrenda populo prenunciavit ; sed quoniam sermones sui a tradicionibus antiquorum sapientium similiter et a via veritatis omnino semoti, indignos memoria eos putavi. Dicebat quidem, caudam comete moveri motu simili motui martis in

epiciclo, ex quo plura nitebatur concludere. Sed quoniam, ut poste-
rius dicitur, ipsa minus mobilis erat capite comete, imo etiam semper
versus occidentem verum [quid]em ex circumvolucione ejus promo-
tum diurno cauda ipsius quandoque respiciebat orientem, sed nunquam
movebatur versus orientem. Etiam uno die omnes differencias posi-
cionis mundi respiciebat; mars autem in suo epiciclo nequaquam
ita faciebat. Et forsan nullus planetarum epiciclum habet quod
magis putandum opinor. Dicebant et alii, cometam a suo astro sicut
ferrum a magnete trahi; cui dissonant dicta partis prime de motu
cometarum. Et etiam quoniam motus tractus per lineam fit brevis-
simam. Alio non existenti impedimento continuo mobili ad trahens
approximante. Ipso quoque mobili existenti cum trahente, fixum,
ad modum ligati, detineretur; quoniam ibi finis est motus tractus.
Hæc patent septimo phisicorum libro ad concavum orbis lune delatus
fuisset; horum contrarium experiencia lucidissime edocuit, quoniam
nulli planetarum conabatur ab omnibus. Discedendo ab ecliptica
diversitas, etiam aspectus ejus, ad stellas sibi vicinas, certificavit
ipsum magis distare a concavo orbis lune quam a terra, in triplo ferè.
Aliqui eciam ni" . . . areλ.

Much more matter relative to this comet might have been given,
but, as these notes have already been extended disproportionately
to the length of the text, I reserve them for another occasion.

Cf. MS. Tann. Bodl. 2. fol. 56, r°.

P. 22, l. 10.—Rather=earlier.

P. 23, l. 6-7.—*The viij. day after Michaelmasse.* " About x. of the
cloke afore none, the King come into the Parlement chamber in his
Parlement robes, and on his hed a cap of mayntenaunce, and sat in
his most Royall Majeste, having before hym his Lordes spirituall and
temporall, and also the speker of the Parlement, which is called
William Alyngton."—MS. Bib. Cotton. Jul. C. vi. fol. 255, r°.

—— *l.* 25.—Axes=Aches.

—— *l.* 33.—*Womere.* So in MS. but should be *wemere.*

P. 24, l. 4.—*A tokene of derthe.* See *Mr. Thoms's Anecdotes and*

Traditions (p. 122), for one instance of this curious superstition; Mr. Thoms refers to Grimm's Mythology for more examples.

P. 24, *l.* 13.—*Lavesham*, i. e. Lewisham.

—— *l.* 15.—*Suthsex.* A mistake in MS. for *Surrey.*

—— *l.* 20.—*A pytte in Kent, in Langley Parke.* This is probably the place where the small stream mentioned in Hasted's History of Kent (II. 140.) took its rise, and joins the river Medway on the south side of it, about half a mile above Maidstone.

—— *l.* 23.—*And this yere he is drye.* This passage shows that these notes of prognosticative prodigies were penned in the same year in which they happened.

P. 25. *l.* 12.—*Hade purchased and byllede.* Moor Park in Hertfordshire, now the seat of the Marquess of Westminster. Clutterbuck (History of Hertfordshire, i. 191) states that the Archbishop had license to inclose 600 acres of pasture and land in Rickmersworth and Watford for a park, and to embattle the site of the manor of Moor in Rickmersworth; and quotes for authority Pat. 9. H. VI. m. 10; but George Neville was then unborn, and on further inquiry we find that the grant was made five years earlier, to Henry (Beaufort) Bishop of Winchester: " Quod Henr' Ep'us Winton' et alii possint kernell' manerium suam de More in Rickmansworth, ac imparcare sexcent, acras terræ, &c. ac liber' warrenn ' ib'm." 2 Pat. 4 Hen. VI. m. 10.—J. G. N.

P. 26, *l.* 16.—*Thens into Fraunce asailed.* i. e. sailed thence into France.

—— *l.* 24.—*xx^{ti}. score men save iij.* William of Worcester, who is probably correct, says only eighty men (*Itin.* 122.);—" memorandum quod comes de Oxford per quinque annos preteritos die Martis in crastino Sancti Michaelis, tempore quo Fortescue armig. fuit vicecomes Cornubiæ, applicuit ad castrum Mont Mychelle cum LXXX hominibus. Et contra XI millia hominum armatorum ex parte domini Regis Edwardi quarti dictum comitem obsedebant per XXIII septimanas, videlicet usque diem sabbati proxima ante diem martis car-

niprivii voc. *le clansyng days* pro . . . . . cum domino Rege demittebat
fortalicium eundo ad dominum Regem."

P. 27, *l.* 5.—*xx. xiij.*—A mistake in MS. for xxiij.

—— *l.* 11.—*comaunde,* i. e. communed.

It was only at the eleventh hour that I was informed that the first
notice I have inserted (Introd. p. viii.) of the death of Henry VI.
has been previously printed by Sir Frederick Madden in the *Collectanea Topographica et Genealogica,* i. 278, 280.

I may also observe that Merlin's prophecy of *bellum inter duos dra-
cones, videlicet album et rubeum,* was completely fulfilled in the wars of
the Roses.—Cf. MS. Cotton. Vespas. B. x. fol. 23, v⁰.

INDEX.

Also published by
LLANERCH:

THE CHRONICLE OF
ADAM OF USK.

A HISTORY OF THE KINGS
by Florence of Worcester.

CONTEMPORARY CHRONICLES
OF THE MIDDLE AGES
by William of Malmesbury,
Richard of Hexham,
and Jordan Fantasme.

TALIESIN POEMS
trans. M. Pennar.

THE BLACK BOOK
OF CARMARTHEN
trans. M. Pennar.

From booksellers.
Write for a complete list
to: Llanerch Enterprises,
Felinfach, Lampeter,
Dyfed Sa488PJ